Toxic Masculinity

Other Books of Related Interest

Opposing Viewpoints Series

Identity Politics
Mass Incarceration
Violent Video Games and Society
Western Democracy at Risk

At Issue Series

Campus Sexual Violence
Domestic Terrorism
Gender Politics
Populism in the Digital Age

Current Controversies Series

Bullying
Microaggressions, Safe Spaces, and Trigger Warnings
Political Correctness
Political Extremism in the United States

> “Congress shall make no law … abridging the freedom of speech, or of the press.”
>
> ***First Amendment to the US Constitution***

The basic foundation of our democracy is the First Amendment guarantee of freedom of expression. The Opposing Viewpoints series is dedicated to the concept of this basic freedom and the idea that it is more important to practice it than to enshrine it.

Toxic Masculinity

Barbara Krasner, Book Editor

Published in 2020 by Greenhaven Publishing, LLC
353 3rd Avenue, Suite 255, New York, NY 10010

First Edition

Articles in Greenhaven Publishing anthologies are often edited for length to meet page requirements. In addition, original titles of these works are changed to clearly present the main thesis and to explicitly indicate the author's opinion. Every effort is made to ensure that Greenhaven Publishing accurately reflects the original intent of the authors. Every effort has been made to trace the owners of the copyrighted material.

Cover image: Imgorthand/E+/Getty Images

Library of Congress Cataloging-in-Publication Data

Names: Krasner, Barbara, editor.
Title: Toxic masculinity / Barbara Krasner, book editor.
Description: First edition. | New York : Greenhaven Publishing, 2020. | Series: Opposing viewpoints | Includes bibliographical references and index. | Audience: Grades 9–12.
Identifiers: LCCN 2018059180| ISBN 9781534505049 (library bound) | ISBN 9781534505056 (pbk.)
Subjects: LCSH: Masculinity—Juvenile literature. | Aggressiveness—Juvenile literature. | Men—Identity—Juvenile literature.
Classification: LCC BF692.5 .T69 2020 | DDC 305.31—dc23
LC record available at https://lccn.loc.gov/2018059180

Manufactured in the United States of America

Website: http://greenhavenpublishing.com

Contents

The Importance of Opposing Viewpoints

Perhaps every generation experiences a period in time in which the populace seems especially polarized, starkly divided on the important issues of the day and gravitating toward the far ends of the political spectrum and away from a consensus-facilitating middle ground. The world that today's students are growing up in and that they will soon enter into as active and engaged citizens is deeply fragmented in just this way. Issues relating to terrorism, immigration, women's rights, minority rights, race relations, health care, taxation, wealth and poverty, the environment, policing, military intervention, the proper role of government—in some ways, perennial issues that are freshly and uniquely urgent and vital with each new generation—are currently roiling the world.

If we are to foster a knowledgeable, responsible, active, and engaged citizenry among today's youth, we must provide them with the intellectual, interpretive, and critical-thinking tools and experience necessary to make sense of the world around them and of the all-important debates and arguments that inform it. After all, the outcome of these debates will in large measure determine the future course, prospects, and outcomes of the world and its peoples, particularly its youth. If they are to become successful members of society and productive and informed citizens, students need to learn how to evaluate the strengths and weaknesses of someone else's arguments, how to sift fact from opinion and fallacy, and how to test the relative merits and validity of their own opinions against the known facts and the best possible available information. The landmark series Opposing Viewpoints has been providing students with just such critical-thinking skills and exposure to the debates surrounding society's most urgent contemporary issues for many years, and it continues to serve this essential role with undiminished commitment, care, and rigor.

The key to the series's success in achieving its goal of sharpening students' critical-thinking and analytic skills resides in its title—

Opposing Viewpoints. In every intriguing, compelling, and engaging volume of this series, readers are presented with the widest possible spectrum of distinct viewpoints, expert opinions, and informed argumentation and commentary, supplied by some of today's leading academics, thinkers, analysts, politicians, policy makers, economists, activists, change agents, and advocates. Every opinion and argument anthologized here is presented objectively and accorded respect. There is no editorializing in any introductory text or in the arrangement and order of the pieces. No piece is included as a "straw man," an easy ideological target for cheap point-scoring. As wide and inclusive a range of viewpoints as possible is offered, with no privileging of one particular political ideology or cultural perspective over another. It is left to each individual reader to evaluate the relative merits of each argument—as he or she sees it, and with the use of ever-growing critical-thinking skills—and grapple with his or her own assumptions, beliefs, and perspectives to determine how convincing or successful any given argument is and how the reader's own stance on the issue may be modified or altered in response to it.

This process is facilitated and supported by volume, chapter, and selection introductions that provide readers with the essential context they need to begin engaging with the spotlighted issues, with the debates surrounding them, and with their own perhaps shifting or nascent opinions on them. In addition, guided reading and discussion questions encourage readers to determine the authors' point of view and purpose, interrogate and analyze the various arguments and their rhetoric and structure, evaluate the arguments' strengths and weaknesses, test their claims against available facts and evidence, judge the validity of the reasoning, and bring into clearer, sharper focus the reader's own beliefs and conclusions and how they may differ from or align with those in the collection or those of their classmates.

Research has shown that reading comprehension skills improve dramatically when students are provided with compelling, intriguing, and relevant "discussable" texts. The subject matter of these collections could not be more compelling, intriguing, or urgently relevant to today's students and the world they are poised to inherit. The anthologized articles and the reading and discussion questions that are included with them also provide the basis for stimulating, lively, and passionate classroom debates. Students who are compelled to anticipate objections to their own argument and identify the flaws in those of an opponent read more carefully, think more critically, and steep themselves in relevant context, facts, and information more thoroughly. In short, using discussable text of the kind provided by every single volume in the Opposing Viewpoints series encourages close reading, facilitates reading comprehension, fosters research, strengthens critical thinking, and greatly enlivens and energizes classroom discussion and participation. The entire learning process is deepened, extended, and strengthened.

For all of these reasons, Opposing Viewpoints continues to be exactly the right resource at exactly the right time—when we most need to provide readers with the critical-thinking tools and skills that will not only serve them well in school but also in their careers and their daily lives as decision-making family members, community members, and citizens. This series encourages respectful engagement with and analysis of opposing viewpoints and fosters a resulting increase in the strength and rigor of one's own opinions and stances. As such, it helps make readers "future ready," and that readiness will pay rich dividends for the readers themselves, for the citizenry, for our society, and for the world at large.

Introduction

> "*We are born male or female, but not masculine or feminine.*"
>
> —*Sandra Lee Bartky,*
> Femininity and Domination: Studies in the Phenomenology of Depression

A Pew Research Center poll recently concluded that 53 percent of Americans say society looks up to men who are manly or masculine.[1] Sixty percent of those people think looking up to these men is a good thing. Yet, the media remind us daily that there are limits to the idealization of masculinity. Incarceration statistics tell us that a perpetrator of violence is likely a man. According to 2015 statistics from the Federal Bureau of Prisons, 93 percent of those incarcerated are men.[2] Masculinity and its connection to aggression and violence constantly challenge us.

No one knows for sure just who coined the term "toxic masculinity." Some believe psychologists came up with it to describe aggressive and violent behavior of males toward themselves, other men, women, and children. Still others maintain women came up with the term to justify discrimination. One thing is clear: toxic masculinity is a topic of hot debate, exemplified by the recent #MeToo movement in which women have been speaking up about sexual harassment and the response to #MeToo by #NotAllMen, which asserts not all men behave in this way. Scholars and journalists wonder, though, whether toxic masculinity truly exists as they examine the roots of aggression and anger. They also explore how socially constructed gender traits, masculine or feminine, can be harmful to all. Toxic femininity, for example, refers to women who demonstrate meanness, and a lack of willingness to nurture and to cooperate.

Cultural norms may dictate how we think of men and women, their traits, and their roles. "Boys will be boys" has been used as a justification for bad behavior. The terms male and female describe biological sex. However, gender is a social construct, and that plays into the social underpinnings of toxic masculinity. A male need not be masculine, for example, to be a man, some will argue. But societal norms insist that boys and men need to show strength, an interest in sex, leadership, and strong earning power. They must not show emotion, vulnerability, or an interest in household chores, parenting, or raising children. If they do not show the proper traits, they can feel emasculated.

Toxic masculinity, however, can be more than a label. It can be a disease. Men can suffer from toxic masculinity and they deserve help and attention. The issue, though, is that the label of "masculine" may prohibit men in desperate need of help from seeking any. They have been taught to hold back emotion and not express themselves verbally when they're in pain. Yet, if they have learned to "man up" and "to be a man," without showing any signs of weakness, they cannot get support. In the end, this behavior is only harmful to them and those surrounding them. Toxic masculinity, then, is literally killing these men whether they are victims or perpetrators. The three-year "Men's Project" at Duke University found that "toxic masculinity" creates rape culture, violence, and oppression online.[3] Questions still remain about whether "masculinity" leads to mass shootings and abuse or whether mental illness is the cause, irrespective of gender. Longevity studies continue to reveal that males have a shorter lifespan. Is toxic masculinity to blame?

Straying from the norm can create feelings among boys that they do not or cannot measure up. They may be called "wuss," "wimp," or "girl." These values may also be communicated through the media, especially advertising. A lack of self-esteem may build up and could result in withdrawal or aggression to overcompensate and fulfill the expectations society has of them.

Key to understanding toxic masculinity is being open to the idea of healthy masculinity and celebrating the diversity of masculinity that is not harmful to anyone. Conversations about toxic masculinity may even lead to this kind of open-mindedness. Educators have a role to play, according to some pundits. Teachers should, for example, enforce the notion that there is room for boys to show and feel tenderness without affecting their masculinity. They should put a stop where they can to name-calling and labeling. Ultimately, they should teach gender equality for all.

Opposing Viewpoints: Toxic Masculinity examines all sides of the issues in chapters titled, "Does Toxic Masculinity Exist?," "Does Toxic Masculinity Represent a Cultural Norm?," "Is It Necessary for Males to Demonstrate Aggression?," and "Does Toxic Masculinity Only Affect Men?" These questions address cultural, sociological, biological, neurological, and ethical issues debated by leading scholars, researchers, and journalists.

Notes

1. Pew Research Center, "Americans See Society Placing More of a Premium on Masculinity Than on Femininity," December 5, 2017. http://www.pewsocialtrends.org/2017/12/05/americans-see-society-placing-more-of-a-premium-on-masculinity-than-on-femininity/.
2. Dyfed Loesche, "The Prison Gender Gap," Statista: The Statistics Portal, October 23, 2017. https://www.statista.com/chart/11573/gender-of-inmates-in-us-federal-prisons-and-general-population/.
3. Study International Staff, "US: Toxic Masculinity Is Being Tackled at Duke University," SI, January 26, 2018, accessed September 30, 2018, https://www.studyinternational.com/news/us-toxic-masculinity-tackled-duke-university/.

Chapter 1

Does Toxic Masculinity Exist?

Chapter Preface

Since the news of Hollywood producer Harvey Weinstein's acts of sexual harassment hit the media in the fall of 2017, women have come forward claiming #metoo and identifying their perpetrators. This harassment has been linked with toxic masculinity behaviors that include aggression and dominance over women. Debates continue over the source of the term and whether men or women created it. Either way, toxic masculinity has gained major media attention.

Even with the use of the Merriam-Webster dictionary and internet searches, defining the exact nature of toxic masculinity proves challenging. Definitions may simultaneously adhere to and defy traditional stereotypes. These stereotypes receive reinforcement from books, newspapers, movies, and social media. At the same time, these same media can demonstrate a new "tender" kind of masculinity that exudes layers and nuances. Behaviors need to be understood before interventions can happen.

University campuses have developed research and student life projects to help promote the idea of healthy masculinity. But some of these programs come under attack for communicating inconsistent messages. However, a more fundamental question is whether toxic masculinity is a mental health issue. Some psychologists believe it is and that it can be effectively treated through therapy. If men are able to learn how to express their emotions, they can begin to understand the multiple dimensions of what it means to be a man. However, other psychologists insist toxic masculinity emerges from cultural and social conditioning. One toxic trait, anger, for example, occurs in both men and women. However, studies have found that they express this anger differently. Men show more physical aggression while women hold on to their anger, forming resentment.

The viewpoints in the following chapter examine the roots of the term "toxic masculinity" and how the social construct of gender plays a role in the demonstration of violent behaviors among men.

Viewpoint 1

> *"The need to keep a certain 'pride' by silencing the women—especially the women—who would dare to name the disease is the very thing killing their souls."*

Name the Shame of Toxic Masculinity

Emily C. A. Snyder

In the following viewpoint, Emily C. A. Snyder argues that some women rationalize men's bad behaviors, which include emotional inexpression, devaluing women's opinions, and seeking physical, sexual, and intellectual dominance. The author outlines the derivation of the term "toxic masculinity" and cites personal examples in which she has encountered toxic behavior. She further illustrates her points with a case of a well-known male playwright. Ultimately, Snyder calls for a treatment of love. Emily C. A. Snyder is a New York–based playwright, director, and novelist.

As you read, consider the following questions:

1. Why do men push back on the term "toxic masculinity," according to the viewpoint?
2. How might women reinforce men's toxic behaviors?
3. How is the label of toxic masculinity applied?

"Defining 'Toxic Masculinity' or Terms of Enragement," by Emily C. A. Snyder, emilycasnyder.blogspot.com, December 19, 2017. Reprinted by permission.

An interesting thing happened on the way to blogging today. Yesterday, I began a series of posts which will attempt to deconstruct the complicated knots around toxic masculinity: particularly in light of the recent power abuse scandals, resulting in sexual and physical aggression, primarily although not exclusively against women.

I began the series, perhaps surprisingly, with a history of my own experiences of positive masculinity among my male mentors. Men who raised me up, rather than kept me down. Men who shaped how I view masculinity: which is noble, kind, protective, encouraging, challenging, and virtuous.

I expected to be lambasted for daring to say that there were good men in the world. Instead, I was lambasted by men for saying anything about men at all.

Defining Terms

So, let's start by defining terms. Just what is "toxic masculinity?" Is it a helpful phrase? What exactly are we deconstructing here?

The term "toxic masculinity" appears to have been initially coined by the Mythopoetic Men's Movement (MMM) of the 1980s-90s, which sought to restore the "deep masculine" to modern man. Inspired by the works of Joseph Campbell and Carl Jung, and not to be confused with Tolkien's mythopoeia, the MMM led by Shepherd Bliss used the term "toxic masculinity" to disassociate negative traits among men from the good of masculinity itself.

Things which were deemed toxic to masculinity include:

- Shame, disassociation, and avoidance of emotional expression;
- Extreme self-reliance;
- The over-aspiration for physical, sexual and intellectual dominance;
- The systematic devaluation of women's opinions, body and sense of self; and by extension
- A condemnation of anything "feminine" within another man.

Lingual Appropriation and Retaliation

Since then, the term has been picked up by feminists and has had a recent resurgence in the light of egregious actions done by men, from the sexual misconduct of Louis CK to the apologetics for the same from Matt Damon.

Due to this, there's been a pushback to the term "toxic masculinity" from the modern descendants of the MMM, such as the Menenist movement, #YesAllMen, #NotAllMen, The Red Pill, and others. The pushback has continued through the male apologetics in the conservative right, largely disapproving of the term because of its association to the perceived liberal agenda of the feminist movement.

The usual objection to "toxic masculinity" is that the term may be construed to mean that all men are by nature toxic. Or that masculinity is, at its essence, evil. Of course, for those laboring under this misunderstanding, it's natural that some might object to the term or even deny that toxic masculinity exists. After all, at least in Christian doctrine, all things were created good—including men.

But also in Christian doctrine, all things fell. Including men.

What's Your Poison?

So, by this definition, what does toxic masculinity look like? In my own experience, I've been on the receiving end of overt sexual harassment, as well as systematic sexism in the workplace, too.

Overt sexual harassment—the boy who looked up my skirt, the jock who made unwanted advances for half a year, the Nigerian man in Paris who nearly abducted me, the man on the subway masturbating on the seat across from me—is easy to condemn. It's easy to identify as assault, and therefore easier to press criminal charges. I say "easier," because as we know, it only took several decades before Weinstein's victims were finally believed.

Which brings me to the considerably more insidious toxicity that allowed Weinstein and others to prey on those in their power:

When women's voices are disregarded because they were caught having an opinion while being female.

Take the case of Israel Horovitz, a prominent playwright who sexually abused the young women he was mentoring. Although his misdeeds had already been published in a series of articles in 1993 in *The Boston Phoenix*, the allegations were dismissed. The playwright claimed "character assassination," while the theatre board's then-president called Horovitz' victims, "tightly wound, if you know what I mean." In short, the predator and his accomplice called the women crazy, and everyone believed the predator and his accomplice.

A similar thing happened to me just today. In posting yesterday's article on a few groups on Facebook, I was told by one man that: "Toxic masculinity is a myth... Knock off the divisive BS." While another man (not an author) went to great length to give me advice about how to make my blog more appealing to men, while also calling me "brazen" and saying that it was:

> ...preachy for a woman to tell a man how to be a man, especially without conceding that she isn't a man and couldn't possibly know what that's like. It is additionally awkward when the woman spends a particularly large amount of space talking about how she engages in these authentically masculine activities. It comes across as telling us that you both understand masculinity better than men and actually engage in masculine activities more than men."

When asked for further clarification about what emotional wound I was striking in my article complimenting masculinity, or what "authentically masculine activity" I had usurped, I was told that he couldn't be bothered—at which time, his wife swooped in to scold me for hurting his feelings.

This may not be an example of sexual predation, but it is textbook toxicity. Go back to a few of the symptoms of this particular poison:

- Shame, disassociation, and avoidance of emotional expression;

- The over-aspiration for physical, sexual and intellectual dominance;
- The systematic devaluation of women's opinions, body and sense of self

Curiously, towards the end of the exchange with the second man, I found myself feeling more and more toxic myself. Wanting to hurl such unhelpful invective as: "What? Did I make you cry, girly man? Gotta have your wife come out and tell me to shut up?" You know. Fun internalized misogyny that I carry around, too. Toxicity hurts everyone.

A Few Good Men

But perhaps, O my apparent male readership, you cannot hear what I am saying Because Female. In that case, let me introduce you to Harris O'Malley, aka Dr. Nerdlove, who has this to say about what it's like for a man to carry around internalized misandry. (Section quoted nearly in full, because it's worth reading.) In regards to why "good men" don't believe women when they report being victimized:

"One of the issues with being a 'good' man is that it's definitional. Because we see ourselves as good, we assume that, by default, what we do is good. One of the reasons why sexism and harassment goes unchecked in geek spaces is because geeks often define themselves in contrast to jocks and bullies. Jocks are rape-y, bullying assholes and the opposite of nerds, so clearly nerds can't be bullying, rape-y assholes. Nice Guys are the opposite of those manipulative assholes so clearly they can't possibly be manipulating women to get what they want.

"Once you've defined yourself as being 'one of the good ones,' it's very hard to want to look around and admit that maybe you aren't as good as you could be. Very, very few people like to believe that they might not be the good guy, and so they're invested in not asking too many questions.

"This is why so many men get their backs up when someone points out that they could be doing better. Criticism, even mild criticism, gets taken as a deeply personal attack because hey: you're one of the good ones.

"And that desire to believe in your goodness reflects not just on you but the people you associate with. After all, if you find out that someone in your social circle has been harassing women… well, what does that say about you? You're a good man. You'd never put up with this. But you did. So what does that say about you?

"This doesn't happen at the conscious level. Nobody thinks to themselves 'I'd rather keep my friend who gets drunk and tries to corner women in the bathroom because admitting he's rape-y reflects badly on my choices.' What they do think is that this is their friend. He's shared their secrets. He's invited them to his parties, made them laugh. They've broken bread together and drank beers together. Surely he can't be that bad, right? There has to be a reason that this isn't as bad as it seems.

"And so the rationalization begins. Maybe she was mistaken. She must be exaggerating. He didn't mean it. He's not that bad. It's not him, it's the drinking. It's the drugs. He's going through a bad time.

"It's easier to explain why your problematic friend isn't bad than it is to look around and realize that you need to improve.

"The other, related reason however is that same system that empowers men. Men tend to believe other men above women. Many of these scandals only 'broke' because a man reported on them—despite women shouting about it to the skies. The fact that Bill Cosby was drugging and raping women was an open secret in Hollywood. Multiple women came forward to accuse Cosby and nobody listened or cared. But once Hannibal Buress called him out publicly, the story began to get traction. Many, many women—especially trans women—were shouting about Milo [Yiannopoulos], but again, it took a Buzzfeed article written by a man to finally make everyone sit up and listen.

"This isn't to say that they shouldn't have spoken up. But it's important to acknowledge system [sic] that privileges their voices above the voices (and lived experiences) of their victims."

I recommend reading his blog, although be warned that he doesn't shy away from language. But for those of you struggling with some wound regarding your masculinity, and seething that I might have something to say about it, may I suggest you go see the doctor?

Now to those still remaining...!

A Voice to Be Reckoned With

So, let's engage from afar with man number two. Upon what authority do I speak about the poisons plaguing too many modern men? Well, I speak with the same authority as a mother does to her son, or a sister to her brothers, a teacher to her students, a doctor to her patient. A lover to her beloved.

Because at the end of the day, nothing gets changed without love. Nor do you have any reason to listen to me if you presume I am the enemy, or if I come at you with hatred and a desire for your destruction. No. I desire the restitution—as far as that is possible in this corrupted world—of positive masculinity within men. Just as I desire the restitution of positive femininity within women. (Something that I'm sure I'll be writing about more, soon.)

Nor do I entirely blame those men who see the term "toxic masculinity" and immediately presume they are being personally singled out to be shamed. The very term they dislike is the very thing that haunts them. The shame, and inability to name that shame, is the very poisonous thing being suffered. The need to keep a certain "pride" by silencing the women—especially the women—who would dare to name the disease is the very thing killing their souls. But it can be overcome.

> *"Have we really made the essential cultural shifts that ensure women are no longer the 'second sex,' living in worlds devised, defined and controlled by men?"*

#MeToo Complaints Are Not Enough to Balance Gender Power

Eva Cox

In the following viewpoint, Eva Cox argues that the #MeToo movement sparked by accusations of sexual harassment against American movie producer Harvey Weinstein is not enough to re-balance power among men and women. She points to perpetuating socially constructed beliefs that men should stand up for themselves and women should be nice. These beliefs, she contends, lead to toxic masculinity and passive femininity. Eva Cox is a professorial fellow at the University of Technology Sydney (Australia). She writes often about social issues.

"#MeToo Is Not Enough: It Has Yet to Shift the Power Imbalances That Would Bring About Gender Equality," by Eva Cox, The Conversation Media Group Ltd, 03/19/2018. https://theconversation.com/metoo-is-not-enough-it-has-yet-to-shift-the-power-imbalances-that-would-bring-about-gender-equality-92108.

As you read, consider the following questions:

1. What changes can complaints and social media enact to combat toxic masculinity?
2. What is the difference between individual complaints and group complaints?
3. Can legal process affect social change?

When news of the allegations against Hollywood producer Harvey Weinstein broke last October, it unleashed a torrent of emotion, especially on social media, offering permission to disclose current and past experiences of sexual harassment and assault. In an unprecedented quantum of use, it offered many angry and upset women accessible ways of venting often long-repressed feelings. It also gave rise to the #MeToo movement.

The volume and breadth of the responses raise many serious questions about the presumed "equality" gains of women. Over the past 70 years, after Simone de Beauvoir, Betty Friedan and Germaine Greer started debates that drove the second-wave feminist movement, we have achieved serious changes to our legal status, paid employment, and roles in public life.

However, the torrents of anger and complaints from #MeToo raise issues of whether gender powers have really been redefined, both locally and in most Western countries. Have we really made the essential cultural shifts that ensure women are no longer the "second sex", living in worlds devised, defined and controlled by men?

The intentions of the second wave covered more than making women equal to men (in their terms, as were then defined). We intended to create the changes that allowed women and men to redefine what matters, to ensure we were no longer seen as primarily sexual or reproductive objects.

The current debate is just further evidence we failed to make the necessary power shifts. And macho male resistance to women's power may also be increasing.

The evidence online and increasingly in reports and complaints, plus the intransigent domestic violence numbers, suggest current gender power imbalances are creating far too many damaging and unequal male-female relationships. Too many men, including those in power, express their ego, insecurities, problems and frustrations by dominating, bullying, controlling, undermining and embarrassing women.

The public appetite for equitable social changes seems to be receding, replaced with deteriorating social and political trust alongside growing nostalgia and tribalism. So, there appears to be little hope for more progressive power shifts to create more gender fairness.

There has been some optimism that the volume of protests and outpourings would generate public movements for change. But, like most forms of protest, they offer evidence of problems but fail to tackle the broader causes and how to fix them.

Part of the ongoing problem is the lack of serious cultural change programs that shift structures. The emphasis is still on using the law to handle individual complaints via either conciliation or charges.

Conciliation, when it works, does not allocate blame and is usually confidential, so is not a change agent. If charges are laid, the process often damages the complainant, as they are questioned and often shamed, even if they win. Many lose, and the process really becomes a social change deterrent.

There are multiple recorded problems with the individualised complaints model, as those accused seek to crush or shame accusers. A prime recent example of this is the Barnaby Joyce case and allegations of sexual harassment. When this accusation came to light, the personal details of the female complainant were published, and her desire for confidentiality was ignored.

There are many other stories of how those who seek individual complaints are punished: lost jobs, character assassination, being labelled as "difficult", and so on.

While many of the reports are of serious crimes that need to be reported to police, others range from offensive and annoying to bad, crass, stupid behaviour. What they share are macho power

Hegemonic Masculinity

The term "Toxic Masculinity" emerged from writings on masculinity by Australian sociologist and arguably, the founding mother of Australia's gender studies curriculum, Raewyn Connell. Prior to its first use, the components of its definition were established in Connell's 1985 paper, "Theorizing Gender," which cites existing feminist theory including role theory. In this paper, Connell lays the groundwork for attributing dysfunctional behavior in men to socially imposed gender roles and stereotypes.

Connell later began using the term "Hegemonic Masculinity" to denote a given culture's standard expectations of characteristics to be displayed by men and boys. The usage is based on the Marxist term "Cultural Hegemony," which refers to a ruling class's use of imposition of its worldview as a social norm to dominate an otherwise culturally diverse society. "Hegemonic Masculinity," derived from this theory, was used to establish social expectations of masculine characteristics as both a vehicle for and evidence of male domination of women. "Toxic Masculinity," derived from Hegemonic Masculinity, is a term used to frame dysfunctional characteristics or behavior as gender-specific.

"Toxic Masculinity," by Hannah Wallen, *Honey Badger Brigade*, October 11, 2017.

assumptions and powerless feminised responses, all of which ensures they are inadequately tackled.

Accusations of crimes create often expensive court cases that cause damage to a complainant even if she wins. So, formal justice may offer little relief.

Yes, the system does punish those convicted as perpetrators, but it deters few, as individualised measures do not affect most of the wider societal groups that misuse their macho power.

Legal processes, even if based on rights, do not really effect the serious social change to attitudes or power that real gender equity will require. We need to address the social mores and related power structures that reinforce male power and support toxic masculinity.

How can we use the current explosion of evidence and outrage to trigger the needed changes?

We are still in early days of the "new" media as social change agents. Some positives: celebratory protests at award ceremonies and the wearing of supportive signs and colours have increased media coverage and the visibility of public support. There are discussions of increased resources for legal actions against perpetrators, and for more funding support to care for victims.

But these "solutions" are similar to those being pursued in the many campaigns against domestic violence, helping survivors. While these responses are needed in the short term, we must realise that they will not drive the cultural and gendered power changes we need. If "clicktivism" replaces wider political action and campaigns for change, we go backwards.

If we are serious about the abuse of gender-based power, we must look at its causes and make structural and cultural changes. We must overcome the serious, widespread gender-biased socialisation of boys and girls, in most cases long before they reach puberty.

Basic assumptions about gender roles still create beliefs about being an acceptable boy (stand up for yourself) or girl (be nice and read people's feelings). These offer surefire paths to toxic masculinity and passive femininity.

These emerged in a recent BBC documentary, broadcast on the ABC. It showed seven-year-olds displaying very stereotypical views of preferring male over female when it came to confidence in skills and leadership. It also showed how removing school and home items that reinforced gender roles could reduce the different socialisations—in other words, it's not genetic.

Given all of that, my concern is that #MeToo and related expressions of anger are failing to fix causes that increase macho-driven gender power imbalances. This means we need real, practical solutions to bridge the gender divide and stop supporting toxic masculinity.

Viewpoint 3

> *"Ironically, the men who willed the term toxic masculinity into existence, exhibited signs of it as they censured women for it."*

Toxic Masculinity Fills Google Searches

Tracy E. Gilchrist

In the following viewpoint, Tracy Gilchrist breaks down the definition of "toxic masculinity" and examines the results of Google searches for these and associated key terms. Using examples from current events, the press, and websites, she argues that attitudes must shift about the meanings of masculinity and femininity and move away from restrictive gender stereotypes that are harmful to all. Tracy E. Gilchrist is Feminism Editor for The Advocate *magazine in Los Angeles, California.*

As you read, consider the following questions:

1. What other terms are associated with toxic masculinity, according to the viewpoint?
2. Why would Planned Parenthood advocate for multiple dimensions of masculinity and femininity?
3. What roles have celebrities played in publicizing toxic masculinity?

With the barrage of sexual harassment and assault allegations that have surfaced since the *New York Times* exposed Harvey Weinstein as a serial sexual predator in early October, Google searches for the term "toxic masculinity" have spiked, and several recent online articles have invoked the term. There are those opinion and news pieces that acknowledge toxic masculinity as palpable, dangerous, and solvable like "Toxic Masculinity is Everywhere. It's Up to Us Men to Fix This" in the *Guardian*. And then there are articles that reject the notion of toxic masculinity by conflating it with all masculinity, like a piece Fox News ran titled "Matt Lauer Was Fired a Week Ago for Appalling Behavior, Not 'Toxic Masculinity.'"

Not entirely unlike wind, gravity, and love, toxic masculinity isn't something that can be held in your hands, turned over, and inspected. But despite its intangibility, we know it when we see it from its effects—the lone gunman who massacred crowds of people at a concert in Las Vegas, the Orlando Pulse nightclub shooting (just about any mass shooting), Weinstein, James Toback, Kevin Spacey, and Brett Ratner, and the ubiquitous schoolyard bully who terrorizes the sensitive kid on the playground with taunts of "be a man."

But utter the phrase "toxic masculinity" in certain milieus and inevitably there will be some with a kneejerk #NotAllMen defense—as if "toxic," which Merriam-Webster defines as "containing or being poisonous material especially when capable of causing death or serious debilitation," or "extremely harsh, malicious, or harmful," weren't modifying "masculinity."

Therein lies the problem with attempting to define the term with its hazy etymology, as swaths of those who hear it will decry "fake news" before they can use it in a sentence like, "Donald Trump's unfettered 'toxic masculinity' makes him think he can kiss and grab women 'by the pussy' without consent."

"Every time feminists talk about toxic masculinity, there is a chorus of whiny dudes who will immediately assume—or pretend to assume—that feminists are condemning all masculinity, even though the modifier 'toxic' inherently suggests that there are forms of masculinity that are not toxic," feminism, politics, and culture writer Amanda Marcotte asserted in "Overcompensation Nation: It's Time to Admit That Toxic Masculinity Drives Gun Violence," a response piece to the Orlando massacre that ran on Salon.

To be clear, "toxic" is the modifier, so the term "toxic masculinity" in no way implicates all men or even all masculine people as abusers, harassers, or terrorizers. But because "masculinity" as defined by Merriam-Webster means "having qualities appropriate to or usually associated with a man," has become mutable and difficult to pin down, especially with evolving studies of gender as a construct, it is useful to look at how "toxic masculinity" has historically been defined.

The etymology of the term can be traced not to academia, but to the rise of the Mythopoetic men's movement of the '80s and '90s—a response to the cultural shift second-wave feminism brought about—where men bonded often in the wilderness and in sweat lodges to attempt to rediscover their "deep masculinity." The movement was bolstered in large part by Robert Bly's book *Iron John*, in which he asserted that the feminist movement caused men to examine their feminine sides to the detriment of their male rituals, according to writer and feminist Erin Innes.

"The male in the past twenty years has become more thoughtful, more gentle. But by this process he has not become more free," Bly wrote in the introduction to his deeply heteronormative book *Iron John*, which fails to consider any worldview other than that of mostly middle-class, straight, cisgender white men.

Shepherd Bliss, another figure in the Mythopoetic men's movement, is credited with having coined the phrase "toxic masculinity," asserting that it was the result of modern culture repressing "deep masculinity." And unlike its current use, toxic masculinity, created in 1993 in response to feminism, was primarily concerned with its effects on toxically masculine men.

Mythopoetic figure Frank Pittman further investigated the term in the early '90s and came to the conclusion that toxic masculinity

Why Colleges Should Stop Teaching Toxic Masculinity

On college campuses across the globe, young men are treated to lectures, workshops, and extracurricular activities that teach them their masculinity—an element at the very core of their identity—is dangerous, poisonous, and even *toxic*.

This semester, an incoming freshman and his peers at Gettysburg College were ordered to watch a film on toxic masculinity during student orientation.

And at both Duke University and the University of North Carolina, seminars are now offered for men to deprogram themselves of their so-called "toxic masculinity."

But while the term seems to be first popularized by grassroots writers, particularly by men seeking to raise awareness of male-specific issues, the term has recently been co-opted by the feminist establishment as a way to scapegoat, blame, and denigrate men as a whole.

In the college classroom, toxic masculinity is presented to students as a reality that affects all men, and is harmful to all women.

Most often, this is in Women's Studies or Sociology classes, and it reflects the broader patriarchal framework of viewing men as dangerous and women as helpless victims.

"Why Colleges Should Stop Teaching 'Toxic Masculinity,'" by Toni Airaksinen, Quillette Pty Ltd, November 16, 2016.

resulted from women raising boys without the presence of male role models, thereby blaming women for its existence. But his blame-throwing at women didn't stop there. He wrote:

> Why do men love their masculinity so much? Because men have been taught to sacrifice their lives for their masculinity, and men always know that they are far less masculine than they should be. Women, though, have the power to give a man his masculinity or take it away, so women become both terrifyingly important and terrifyingly dangerous to men.

So, ironically, the men who willed the term toxic masculinity into existence, exhibited signs of it as they censured women for it. Pittman, who was deeply concerned about the deleterious effects of toxic masculinity on men, wrote that men live seven years less than women, suffer higher rates of suicide, homicide, lung cancer, cirrhosis of the liver, and other illnesses, which is all true. But he and the other Mythopoetics failed to truly investigate its effects on those impacted by toxically masculine people.

All of that brings us to more recent attempts to define the term. Marcotte, writing for *Salon*:

> Toxic masculinity is a specific model of manhood, geared toward dominance and control. It's a manhood that views women and LGBT people as inferior, sees sex as an act, not of affection but domination, and which valorizes violence as the way to prove one's self to the world. Toxic masculinity aspires to toughness but is, in fact, an ideology of living in fear: The fear of ever seeming soft, tender, weak, or somehow less than manly. This insecurity is perhaps the most stalwart defining feature of toxic masculinity.

If it weren't enough that Marcotte delivered such a pithy, all-encompassing definition, she also offered current examples:

> Donald Trump flipping out when someone teases him about his small fingers. (Or about anything, really.) The ludicrously long and shaggy beards on "Duck Dynasty," meant to stave off any association with the dreaded feminine with a thicket of hair. The emergence of the term "cuckservative," flung around by hardline right-wingers to suggest that insufficient racism is somehow emasculating. Conservatives absolutely melting down about an Obamacare ad that suggested that, gasp, sometimes men wear pajamas.

Not every example of toxic masculinity is as obvious or extreme as the standard bearers of it like serial predators like Roy Moore and Trump or the white nationalists carrying tiki torches and angrily shouting racist epithets in Charlottesville. Toxic masculinity abounds to such a degree that the terms "manspreading" and "mansplaining" aren't just a part of the vernacular, but fairly acknowledged as universal experiences for those who've encountered such behavior. And, of course, while not all men who "spread" or "splain" are toxic, the solipsism that requires one to take up more space than needed in public or to condescend and exhibit gendered know-it-all behavior, when unchecked, can lead to toxic masculinity.

Google "traits of masculinity" and it's not easy to find examples or definitions that haven't been co-opted by modern men's rights movements that seek to ostensibly "make a man" of all who click those links. Even the results of a study by researcher Y. Joel Wong and his colleagues published in 2016, which found that sexism is bad for men's health, identified 11 typically masculine traits that are harmful to men's mental health, but the study made no distinction between masculinity and toxic masculinity. Those traits included "desire to win," "need for emotional control," "risk-taking," "violence," "power over women," "disdain for homosexuality," and other none-too-favorable markers.

While it's dismaying that finding positive definitions or defining traits of masculinity is difficult, the same can be said when one Googles "traits of femininity." Searches for that term yield a few feel-good women's empowerment articles and plenty of "how to please your man" pieces.

One of the clearest, most concise breakdowns of masculine (and feminine) traits exists in a section on Planned Parenthood's site that skillfully addresses gender stereotypes, even going so far as to define hyperfemininity and hypermasculinity and offering examples of what to do when one encounters gender stereotyping.

"Extreme gender stereotypes are harmful because they don't allow people to fully express themselves and their emotions," according to Planned Parenthood's website. "For example, it's harmful to masculine folks to feel that they're not allowed to cry or express sensitive emotions. And it's harmful to feminine folks to feel that they're not allowed to be independent, smart or assertive. Breaking down gender stereotypes allows everyone to be their best selves."

Shifting attitudes about the nature of gender and a move away from a binary conception of it and from gender stereotypes typified by *Mad Men*–era toxicity appear to be the way forward, away from toxic masculinity and the societal pressures that inspire some men to prove their manliness by acting out in ever-increasingly violent, oppressive, racist, misogynistic, homophobic, and transphobic ways.

VIEWPOINT 4

> *"While research has not yet suggested that different factors trigger men's anger, researchers continue to uncover differences in how men and women experience it."*

Anger Is Not Just a Masculine Trait

Melissa Dittmann

In the following viewpoint, Melissa Dittmann argues that according to a St. John's University survey, men and women registered equal amounts of anger but expressed it differently. Men showed more physical and passive aggression, while women held on to their anger. Neither of these extremes is healthy. Melissa Dittmann is an award-winning American journalist and scholar. She has been a staff writer for the American Psychological Association's monthly magazine, Monitor on Psychology.

As you read, consider the following questions:

1. How important is scientific research to the study of toxic masculinity?
2. How do men and women express anger differently?
3. What do psychologists recommend as techniques to deal with anger and reduce toxicity?

Both men and women are often ashamed of their anger, although it appears they may experience their anger differently, according to ongoing research. For example, gender socialization can affect how men and women handle their anger, researchers have found.

"Both men and women have been poorly served by the gender socialization they have received," says psychologist Sandra Thomas, PhD, a leading researcher in women's anger who has recently also begun studying men's experiences with anger. "Men have been encouraged to be more overt with their anger. If [boys] have a conflict on the playground, they act it out with their fists. Girls have been encouraged to keep their anger down."

Indeed, anger in men is often viewed as "masculine"—it is seen as "manly" when men engage in fistfights or act their anger out physically, notes Thomas, director of the nursing doctoral program at the University of Tennessee, Knoxville. "For girls, acting out in that way is not encouraged," she says. "Women usually get the message that anger is unpleasant and unfeminine." Therefore, their anger may be misdirected in passive-aggressive maneuvers such as sulking or destructive gossip, she says.

In her view, however, neither approach in its extreme is healthy. It is important, Thomas says, for both men and women to be clear and forthright when they are angry and to use problem-solving techniques in dealing with their anger.

"Things are not getting better in anger behavior," notes Thomas, who cites the many incidences today of violence among children. "We need to understand what anger is about before we can intervene effectively."

Differences in Anger Expression

Also needed, researchers say, are efforts to dislodge gender stereotypes about anger. June Tangney, PhD, for example, has called into question common assumptions about women and anger, such as the notion that women have trouble with anger. Women don't have a problem with anger—they just manage it differently, says Tangney, professor of psychology at George Mason University.

Women tend not to be as aggressive as men in expressing anger and tend to talk about their anger more, she says. "They are more proactive and use more problem-solving approaches in discussing a problem with a person they are angry with," says Tangney.

And what makes ordinary women angry day-to-day? In 1993, Thomas conducted the Women's Anger Study, a large-scale investigation involving 535 women between the ages of 25 and 66. The study revealed three common roots to women's anger: powerlessness, injustice and the irresponsibility of other people.

While research has not yet suggested that different factors trigger men's anger, researchers continue to uncover differences in how men and women experience it. Such was that case for Raymond DiGiuseppe, PhD, chair of the psychology department at St. John's University in New York, in his research to develop a new anger disorder scale. In a survey of 1,300 people ages 18 to 90, DiGiuseppe investigated 18 subscales of anger, including how individuals experience their anger, how long the anger lasts and what they get angry about. While he found that differences in men's and women's total anger scores were not significant, he did find differences in the way they experience anger. Specifically, men scored higher on physical aggression, passive aggression and experiences of impulsively dealing with their anger. They also more often had a revenge motive to their anger and scored higher on coercing other people.

Women, on the other hand, were found to be angry longer, more resentful and less likely to express their anger, compared with men. DiGuiseppe found that women used indirect aggression by "writing off" a higher number of people—intending to never speak to them again because of their anger.

Anger slowly decreases with age, DiGiuseppe found, and differences in the domains of anger between the sexes decreases for those older than 50, although men are still more likely to be aggressive and women are still more likely to have longer episodes of anger. DiGiuseppe's research will be published this year by Multi-Health Systems, a Canadian publisher of psychological tests.

Future Directions

Thomas has expanded the scope of her research and replicated some of her studies on American women's anger with women from different countries, such as France and Turkey. She has also conducted a study aimed at understanding the meaning of men's anger. Her research is awaiting publication in the APA journal *Psychology of Men and Masculinity*.

Anger researchers Deborah Cox, PhD, Patricia Van Velsor, PhD, and Joseph Hulgus, PhD, are working to validate an anger diversion model. Cox first developed the model with Sally Stabb, PhD, and Karin H. Bruckner, authors of *The Anger Advantage* (Broadway, 2003). The model holds that when individuals bypass awareness of their anger, the diversion process can cause anger symptoms. In support, the team has found women who either try to mask their anger, or externalize and project their anger irresponsibly, were at higher risk for anxiety, nervousness, tension and panic attacks.

Cox, a Southwest Missouri State University psychologist and assistant professor, hopes that researchers will also apply the anger diversion model to men and boys. "It may be that men are more reinforced for using certain diversion forms over others—and more than women," Cox says. "However, it seems that the underlying process may be the same across genders, and it's one that could be translated, 'Your anger is wrong and should be gotten rid of as soon as possible.'"

To get at such complexities, researchers may need to try new approaches, Cox says. "Much of what we must do demands that we talk to women and men and get their stories about anger, versus testing them in a paper-and-pencil type of format," she explains. "Only through getting people's verbatim stories can we get a real sense of how they interpret their own anger."

Viewpoint 5

> *"The best thing about Tender Masculinity is that it's not only a necessary antidote to our media portrayals of men—it's also already here."*

Tender Masculinity Offers an Alternative to Toxic Masculinity

terra loire

In the following viewpoint, terra loire argues that a new kind of non-toxic, tender masculinity has entered the world stage. She claims that both Nice Guys and Macho Men are toxic in their own ways. She presents a list of Tender Man characteristics that includes healthy expressions of emotion, ability to have male friendships, and an understanding of boundaries. To illustrate her point, she lists and describes characters from books and movies who demonstrate tender masculinity. terra loire is a feminist writer based in Toronto, Canada.

As you read, consider the following questions:

1. Does this author convince you tender masculinity exists?
2. How might a Nice Guy show toxic masculinity traits?
3. How important are books and movies in demonstrating dimensions of masculinity according to the viewpoint?

"In Praise of Tender Masculinity, the New Non-Toxic Way to Be a Man," by terra loire, electricliterature.com, March 14, 2018. Reprinted by permission.

Media representations of masculinity tend to play in two notes: On the left we have Nice Guys and on the right we have Macho Men. Both play into ideas of toxic masculinity in their own ways. Macho Men are emotionally distant, but it's okay because they're buff and men don't have feelings anyway. Whether it's an action hero like *Die Hard*'s John McClane, or a tortured bad boy like *The Breakfast Club*'s Bender or *Wuthering Heights*' Heathcliff, we are conditioned to see their anger issues as passion and their repressed emotions as something romantic for women to "fix." Nice Guys are seen as an antidote, but more often than not, their niceness is performative and in direct relation to their feelings towards a crush. Think of Laurie in *Little Women*, who grows as a character through the help of Jo, but once she turns him down weaponizes all that character growth as leverage to get in her pants. Or Tom from *500 Days of Summer*: He's a charming underdog, but it's not exactly "nice" of him to resent Summer for not meeting his romantic expectations despite her clear communication of her boundaries. In an era where toxic masculinity is utterly overwhelming, we are all desperate for a healthier and more nuanced role.

Enter Tender Masculinity.

While we have mental imagery of Macho Men (buff, distant) and Nice Guys (nerdy, brooding), the characters that embody Tender Masculinity are multi-layered and come from all backgrounds.

Here is a checklist on how to spot a Tender Man:

- Is he invested in all of his relationships, not just romantic ones?
- Does he express his emotions in a healthy way?
- Is self-awareness a concept he's comfortable with?
- Does he commit to personal growth?
- Are boundaries something he is aware of and respects?
- Is he unafraid of male intimacy—for instance, can he express affection for male friends without making a gay joke?

The best thing about Tender Masculinity is that it's not only a necessary antidote to our media portrayals of men—it's also already here. There aren't a lot of Tender Man characters yet, and we'd love to see more, but a few books and movies are promoting this low-swagger, high-emotion ideal. These are the fully realized male characters we need to celebrate and see more of.

Samwise Gamgee—Lord of the Rings

There are many heroes in the Lord of the Rings trilogy, and many are driven by masculine ideals like duty, honor, glory, or a sense of destiny. But Sam is the indisputable—though somewhat reluctant—hero who tops them all, driven by his love for his friend Frodo. Sam is a devoted friend, who does most of the emotional labor throughout the books. He brings us many moments of Tender Masculinity; following Frodo (even when he's pressured not to) because he won't let his friend suffer alone, recognizing and validating the burden of the One Ring, and being able to give a good dose of tough love when necessary. His emotional vulnerability is what makes him relatable, and it's what makes him powerful. That ring would have never seen its fiery end without Sam in the picture.

Juan, Little/Black/Chiron, and Kevin—Moonlight

Moonlight is a breathtaking story for many reasons, one of those being its examination of toxic masculinity and the importance of tenderness. Tender Masculinity is not an identity of perfection; it is true to the human condition in that it is always a work in progress, a journey. The men of *Moonlight* all have difficult backgrounds, and at times succumb to the pressure of society's poisonous expectations of men, but the moments of beauty in the film are when they embrace tenderness. *Moonlight* takes us through the life of our hero in three major periods: childhood, adolescence, and adulthood. During these periods, we explore his relationship with Juan, his father figure, and his complex feelings for his friend—and eventual lover—Kevin. When we see Juan teach Little how to swim, we're shown the power in tenderness between men. We're shown an important alternative to how the media often portrays masculinity, especially black masculinity. We're shown the value of male friendships that we too often ignore.

Kyle Valenti—Roswell

Kyle Valenti is a high school jock, a type of character usually portrayed as either a cool Macho Man or a bullying meathead who keeps our misfit Nice Guy hero away from the girl of his dreams. In the pilot of *Roswell*, we naturally expect that Kyle, our heroine Liz's sporty main squeeze, will step in with all the fury of the spurned jock when she leaves him behind for the mysterious world surrounding social outcast Max. When we see Max get beat up by Kyle's fellow football players, we assume Kyle told them to. But in fact, Kyle is livid when he finds out what his bros did. He apologizes to Max, and then approaches Liz and expresses his need for more open communication in their relationship.

Usually, the high school jock exits after the first act, but Kyle's tenderness and surprising emotional maturity made him a character fascinating enough to keep around all the way through to the series finale. On this journey we get to see Kyle become a trustworthy ally, a good friend, a hard worker, a devoted son, and an occasional Buddhist. Kyle Valenti was a surprising character to see on mainstream TV in the early aughts, which is what made him so compelling.

Jared—Son of a Trickster

Son of a Trickster, the first book in an in-progress trilogy from Eden Robinson, introduces us to Jared, a 16-year-old Indigenous boy on the cusp of discovering who he really is. We get a full picture of Jared's life; his relationship with his family, a girl next door, friends at school, his neighbors, his dog, and his enemies. Each relationship has its ups and downs throughout Jared's journey, during which he is forced to reexamine his identity, his culture, and his connection to the past. Robinson's novel examines teen angst, while also dispelling stereotypes and misconceptions of Indigenous communities (and Indigenous men in particular) through Jared's story. While Jared sometimes emotionally shuts off, or finds himself in hypermasculine situations, Robinson makes clear that he is still just a child who has a tender side as well. There are many examples of this, but to me the most heartbreaking is how Jared reacts to the death of his dog, which comes at a particularly hectic time in his life. To me, this was the turning point in the novel where Jared allows himself to fully feel, to wallow in his sadness, and this newfound tenderness impacts his actions through the remainder of the story. The end of the book makes clear that diving into his emotions and reevaluating his identity are key to tapping into his magic.

Remus Lupin—Harry Potter

Hogwarts professor and secret werewolf Remus Lupin was the most emotionally mature male in the Harry Potter series, and I will hear no arguments. Though Lupin's lycanthropy initially makes Harry and his friends suspicious, he is shown to be a father figure, a sincere educator, a good friend, and a public-minded citizen committed to protecting his wider community. His most compelling relationship is with Nymphadora Tonks, his wife and the mother of his son. What makes their relationship refreshing is that it does not fit into a cookie cutter soul-mate narrative; their history together is fraught with trauma and grief, but rather than becoming codependent or distant, Lupin takes time to articulate and work through his complex feelings before marrying Tonks. (We won't talk about what happens next.) There are a lot of characters in the Harry Potter series who are heroic through a sense of duty, honor, or sometimes even reluctance, but Lupin is heroic through his tender heart.

Everybody—Magic Mike XXL

Let me tell you, the real magic of this movie isn't the well-choreographed thrusting, it's the celebration of male friendship. In a movie that could be completely cliché, this bro squad does not succumb to the macho stereotypes you may expect. These men are here for each other through thick and thin: relationship problems, supporting healthy sexuality, resisting toxic masculinity, encouraging career goals, and fostering overall personal development. In one of the most GIFable scenes in cinematic history, the friends are reexamining their acts for StripCon (and, yes, rolling on ecstasy). Mike is encouraging the gang to leave behind their cliché personas (fireman, etc.) and develop routines that are representative of themselves. His buddy Big Dick Richie is feeling insecure about coming up with something completely new; he'd rather just stick to his comfort zone instead of putting himself out there. The guys stop at a gas station, and as a way to convince Richie that he is talented at what he does, they challenge him to do a spontaneous number for the incredibly bored gas station employee and give her a reason to smile. While Richie does his improvised routine to a fortuitous Backstreet Boys soundtrack, the rest of his friends are outside cheering him on, genuinely excited to see him gain his confidence back. And Richie succeeds: the woman breaks out in laughter and the boys are re-committed to their vision.

While there are more examples we could list here (all of the men and boys of *Stranger Things*, for example), there is no ignoring that Tender Masculinity is underrepresented in the stories we tell. It is important that we embrace these stories, because while examining toxic male archetypes in media is necessary, condemning them without offering a healthy alternative just leads to more toxic men in media… and in real life. While the idea of tender masculinity is not new, these stories are becoming more mainstream and embraced. But they're rare in the grand scheme of things. If we don't celebrate the ones we have, we risk losing these stories to the same old clichés. Celebrating tender men trickles over into our day-to-day, giving the next generation the male role models they deserve. I look forward to the day when the tender men of fiction are just as common as the Macho Men and Nice Guys we know too well.

> *"Gender does not discriminate when it comes to mental health difficulties, and being a man makes no difference to whether you should feel able to discuss, think about or engage with your feelings."*

Toxic Masculinity Is a Mental Health Problem

Joshua Miles

In the following viewpoint, Joshua Miles argues that toxic masculinity is a mental health issue that can be effectively treated through therapy. He examines the reasons why men find it difficult to talk about their feelings, including the stigma of shame. If men open up and express their emotions, they can begin to realize and fulfill the complexities of being a man. Joshua Miles is an integrative psychotherapist with a practice in East London, UK.

As you read, consider the following questions:

1. How does this author characterize toxic masculinity as a mental health issue?
2. How important is it for men to express their feelings?
3. According to this viewpoint, why does the idea that men are to remain strong, silent, and capable a total myth?

Due to the way young boys are socialised in education and in society, their ability to deal with emotions has been systematically undermined from a young age. Men are taught that certain aspects of their personality are not acceptable, they are taught not to cry or express in words, how they are feeling. In school, they're shown there are certain games they should play, activities they should take part in, and rarely are they encouraged to engage in their feelings.

Television and advertising are a large part of the issue, due to the picture they paint of what a "real man" looks like. Men are bombarded by images and perceptions of masculinity, muscles and bravado, and slowly over time, they are made to believe that being a man entails specific criteria. If they do not tick certain boxes, they are not "man enough."

These perceptions of masculinity can lead to a deep sense of shame permeating throughout male culture. The perceived definition of what it means to be a man is not only outdated and ridiculous, but harmful, not only for the men of today, but those of the future, who see this as the only way of being. The idea that men are to remain strong, silent and capable is a total myth, and belongs more in 1917, than 2017.

Why Don't Men Discuss Their Feelings or Emotions?

Over 3 million men in the UK have a mental health difficulty, and the charity Mind previously found that 37% of men in the UK feel worried or low. The top three issues playing on their minds were job security, work and money.

So, what is the cause of such high numbers of men experiencing mental health difficulties, and why do they find it so difficult to discuss? Here are some common reasons that men may find it difficult to speak about their issues.

- Men often stigmatise themselves, leading to a deep sense of shame about having a mental health difficulty

- Men are often embarrassed to admit to others that they struggle, even if their troubles are considerable, and struggle to seek help
- Men often "put up" with relatively minor difficulties, meaning these can become larger difficulties
- Men often don't display traditional symptoms of mental health difficulties, and may instead "act out," through drug use, alcohol or aggression
- All of these factors can lead to mental health difficulties being undiagnosed or overlooked

Men and Suicide

According to the office of national statistics, the ratio of male to female suicides has shown a sustained rise over the last 30 years. In 1981, 62% of suicides in the UK were male, and in 2014 this figure had risen to 76%. Suicide is the single biggest cause of death in men under the age of 45 in the UK.

So, why are the statistics for male suicide so high? Men have been conditioned to be less in touch with their emotions, or to feel shame or weakness in accessing support, and often feel they have an image to uphold, or fear someone (another man) may find out their weakness.

As such, men do not often feel comfortable in expressing how they feel even if they are having a bad time, because of the expectations of manliness, meaning they feel they should be strong at all times. Not doing so, essentially equates to them feeling as if they have failed as a man.

Masculinity and Feelings

Masculinity, and what it means to be a man, has been implanted, grown and developed in the minds of men since their childhood. Men witness to the stereotypes of masculine heroes, who are self-sufficient, strong and capable. Often the role of offering emotional support is not one associated with being manly, and is therefore dismissed.

Clarifying the Term

"Toxic masculinity" is tricky. It's a phrase that—misunderstood—can seem wildly insulting, even bigoted. Recently, after tweeting about toxic masculinity and its relationship to violence, I ended up the topic of discussion on a major nightly news show and the recipient of the online harassment that regularly follows such discussions these days. Because the term requires careful contextualization and provokes such strong reactions, our impulse may be to avoid discussing it with our classes. As educators, however, it is our responsibility not to hide from difficult topics or concepts, but to clarify them.

The stakes of this conversation couldn't be higher. When we talk about toxic masculinity, we do so not to insult or to injure. If we can talk with students as they are forming their ideas about gender, we can perhaps spare them from thinking that there is only one way to be a man—or any other gendered identity, for that matter—and give them the space to express their gender in ways that feel authentic and safe for themselves. When we talk about toxic masculinity, we are doing so out of love for the boys and men in all of our lives.

"What We Mean When We Say, 'Toxic Masculinity,'" by Colleen Clemens, Southern Poverty Law Center, December 11, 2017.

It is crucial men are able to have conversations with other men about their mental health and feelings, because it is only when the idea of "what it means to be a man" begins to change, that men will be able to open up, or reveal about themselves, those feelings or difficulties they are experiencing.

How Therapy Can Help

It would be wrong to say that men do not ever seek help, or that all men are strong, silent and dismissive of feelings. However, often it is not until a point of crisis that men seek help, leaving things until they are unable to manage them anymore. It is in these points where many men find themselves in therapy, brought about through a relationship difficulty, an issue with stress or an incident at work. It is crucial to recognise, given the past conditioning and perceptions of being a man, this has been an incredibly hard thing to do and accepting they need support is a huge step.

Therapy can offer men the chance to be seen without judgement as they are. They can be seen as vulnerable, stressed, and anxious as well as strong, confident and capable. They will not be told to "man up." In therapy, men can learn to understand more of themselves, their difficulties and their thoughts, and explore the rich and diverse nature of masculinity, and see that it is not a one-sided image so frequently painted by the media. Therapy offers men the chance to explore their pain and difficulty, and to ultimately, be more enriched, and enhanced, and to understand more what it means to be a man.

The importance of dispelling the myths surrounding mental health is crucial for society as a whole, as it allows for a more open and honest conversation to take place and lessen stigma and discrimination. The reality is, mental health operates on a scale, and we all struggle at points.

Gender does not discriminate when it comes to mental health difficulties, and being a man makes no difference to whether you should feel able to discuss, think about or engage with your feelings.

Periodical and Internet Sources Bibliography

The following articles have been selected to supplement the diverse views presented in this chapter.

Hayley Gleeson, "Toxic Masculinity: Will the 'War on Men' Only Backfire?" ABC News, January 27, 2017, https://www.abc.net.au/news/2017-01-28/toxic-masculinity-war-could-backfire/8207704.

Mark Greene, "Why Calling It 'Toxic Masculinity' Isn't Helping," *Medium*, August 11, 2018, https://medium.com/s/man-interrupted/why-we-must-stop-saying-toxic-masculinity-cfe83b9034dc.

Michael Kimmel and Lisa Wade, "Ask a Feminist: Michael Kimmel and Lisa Wade Discuss Toxic Masculinity," *Signs*, 2018, http://signsjournal.org/kimmel-wade-toxic-masculinity/.

Sally Kohn, "We Need 'Extreme Vetting' for Toxic Masculinity," CNN, November 10, 2017, https://www.cnn.com/2017/11/09/opinions/we-need-extreme-vetting-for-toxic-masculinity-kohn/index.html.

Frank Miniter, "The Hard Adrenaline-Soaked Truth about 'Toxic Masculinity,'" *Forbes*, January 18, 2017, https://www.forbes.com/sites/frankminiter/2017/01/18/the-hard-adrenaline-soaked-truth-about-toxic-masculinity/#460d52a82be5.

Lauren Oyler, "When Did Everything Get So 'Toxic'?" *The New York Times Magazine*, October 2, 2018, https://www.nytimes.com/2018/10/02/magazine/when-did-everything-get-so-toxic.html/.

Gad Saad, "Is Toxic Masculinity a Valid Concept?" *Psychology Today*, March 8, 2018, https://www.psychologytoday.com/us/blog/homo-consumericus/201803/is-toxic-masculinity-valid-concept.

Ben Shapiro, "The 'Toxic Masculinity' Smear," *National Review*, June 7, 2017, https://www.nationalreview.com/2017/06/masculinity-not-toxic-stop-blaming-men-everything/.

Samuel Veissière, "The Real Problem with 'Toxic Masculinity,'" *Psychology Today*, February 16, 2018, https://www.psychologytoday.com/us/blog/culture-mind-and-brain/201802/the-real-problem-toxic-masculinity.

Chapter 2

Does Toxic Masculinity Represent a Cultural Norm?

Chapter Preface

Questions arise as to whether gender-based differences and toxic or hegemonic masculinity are social or biological constructs. If they are social, that means that boys learn that acts of aggression and violence are acceptable and are even expected behaviors at home and in school. They are conditioned to play hardball, for example, while girls in their classes or at home are expected to help in the kitchen or play much milder games.

There is also a question of whether certain segments of the population are able to demonstrate toxic behaviors without repercussions while others are not. For instance, does wealth excuse violent and dominant behavior? Without knowing it, parents and teachers may reinforce toxic traits and gender inequality. Through training and education, they may become aware of their own biases.

This conditioning may have roots in the Victorian period when there was a focus on physical prowess. Perhaps then it was necessary to prove oneself in the name of the British Empire in war. Oppressive masculinity, another term for toxic masculinity, some believe, can only result in more violence and more war. However, some experts believe that a pattern of toxic behavior can be broken through open conversation. Such sharing of feelings and stories could help in the healing process for all concerned. The ability of both men and women to accept multiple forms of masculinity becomes important for the healing process as well.

Issues of norms and standards infiltrate environments ranging from the inner sanctum of the home, to school, to the workplace, and to national and international negotiations. Left unchecked, toxic masculinity can affect the entire world. The viewpoints in this chapter examine the existence and nature of social norms regarding toxic masculinity. Viewpoint authors address adolescent behavior in both boys and girls, the learning process, and the acceptability of violent behavior, as well as the role of teachers and parents in shaping these norms.

Viewpoint 1

> *"In order for us to begin breaking down these damaging ideas of masculinity, we as a society have to stop seeing femininity as the weaker end of the dichotomous male-female structure."*

Drop the Man Card and Stop Policing Masculinity

Cara Nicole

In the following viewpoint, Cara Nicole argues that ideas of masculinity and femininity need to be expanded to get beyond stereotypes and tropes. She cites the example of Hollywood superstar Dwayne Johnson (a.k.a. "The Rock"), who has been able to show on screen other forms of masculinity like donning glittery tights. She examines the limitations of the so-called Man Card that can be taken away in a moment if deviation from the standard emerges. Cara Nicole is a student and contributor to The Huffington Post.

"You Don't Have to Be Masculine to Be a Man," by Cara Nicole, Huffingtonpost, June 15, 2016. Reprinted by permission.

As you read, consider the following questions:

1. What problems are associated with the "Man Card," according to the viewpoint?
2. What are the standard tropes that describe this Man Card?
3. According to this viewpoint, how do cultural norms contribute to gender tropes?

Man Card. Noun. Two syllables. Meaning, according to the always helpful Urban Dictionary, the "Requirement to be accepted as a respectable member of the male community." To further understand the phenomenon, one can drop by the "Official Man Card" website, where you can see the latest examples of the "lack of manliness" like "buying a Prius," "crying," or the ever-ambiguous "being pussy-whipped." The Man Card is seen as something that can be revoked from a man in question at a moment's notice, symbolically stripping him of his male identity in the face of society. Such nullification occurs primarily in situations in which a man behaves in ways that stray from the preconceived notions of what masculinity is. It is evidence of a shameful deviation from the accepted. Pinterest membership, crying in public, watching romance movies, enjoying pedicures—anything perceived as tiptoeing into the realm of "feminine" is blacklisted.

The problem with the Man Card is not the word itself. If you want to use that phrase, go ahead. I'm not here to police language, but I'm writing this as a way to acknowledge the policing of masculinity in our culture. The idea of the Man Card tugs at a far larger problem that plagues boys and men; it is a problem that leaves males trapped within the confines of labels, cornered within a labyrinth of insecurity and disingenuity.

The Man Card is an idea that manifests from the tropes of manhood and gender normative thinking. According to the tropes, a man must be strong, emotionless, tough, and dominating. His interests are limited to rugged pastimes or violent pursuits.

As for fashion, dark and monochromatic is key, and under no circumstances shall a man be adorned with pinks or frills.

There are some men who have been able to move beyond the public's scrutiny of the Man Card, such as Dwayne Johnson (aka "The Rock"), who frequently adorns tutus and pink bows in his films. However, Johnson achieves this through a combination of his own security, and public acknowledgment. He's not called The Rock because he's an avid geologist (maybe his is, who knows!), but because the man is solid muscle through and through, or hard as a rock. His masculinity, in the eyes of the world, is unquestionable, therefore allowing him more flexibility in his appearance and behavior. It's awesome to see someone like him be so secure with himself that he'll readily throw on glittery tights, but why isn't the same acceptance given to the Average Joe?

You shouldn't have to have biceps the size of a human baby to be recognized as manly. I want normal guys—my classmates, my cousins, my brother, my friends—to not feel paralyzed in their identity because the world is telling them to be Ken, just as women are told to be Barbie. Though *Toy Story 3* fans know even Ken was teased endlessly for his love of fashion and his trendy ascot.

What I find particularly interesting and unsettling is that behaviors that result in the "revoking" of the Man Card always possess a feminine aspect to them. Our society is structured on a dichotomous relationship between masculinity and femininity. Instead of a venn-diagram, we have two spheres of existence pushed as far apart as possible, never allowed to integrate. Masculinity is seen as exclusive to men, and femininity to women. This leaves little room for people to move beyond such antiquated assumptions of what men and women should be, without even touching on issues such as how these stereotypes affect trans men.

Femininity, along with its stereotyped attributes and behaviors, is perceived as weak, frivolous, and menial. Our destructive idea of masculinity is rooted in the idea that to be a woman is to be inferior, that to act and behave like women is undesirable. Women are given greater freedom to be more stereotypically masculine. We aren't judged when we wear pants. It's seen as cool if we like sports and video games (though there is definitely an assumed incompetence of women in those male-dominated spaces, but that's a whole other topic). We even have a trendy name given if we lean more towards stereotypical male interests—Tomboy. Even women, including myself at times, look down on fellow women who we deem as too "girly."

On the other hand, it has yet to become socially acceptable for men to wear dresses in public. Men are ridiculed for having interests in fashion or baking. When a boy leans more towards stereotypical female interests, he is taunted and teased. Growing up, I remember hearing parents concerned over their sons' interests in princesses, thinking a love for Cinderella would "turn their son gay." I remember my aunt teasing my dad over his Pinterest account for baking recipes, saying she had to take his Man Card away because of it. Sibling love of course, yet it pulls at a larger issue.

In order for us to begin breaking down these damaging ideas of masculinity, we as a society have to stop seeing femininity as the weaker end of the dichotomous male-female structure. Instead of two separate arenas of existence, let us reimagine femininity and masculinity. Instead of being either a masculine person or a feminine person, let us see ourselves like a jar of sand art that holds beautiful blends of colors, a fantastic collision of pinks and blues. With the emergence of terms like Gender Fluid, and Trans rights becoming a real social issue in the past few years, this is already happening, but it's not enough.

For those who still feel resistant to my argument because they think I am calling for an end to men, hear me out. I am not saying every man has to like skirts and Pinterest and winged eyeliner. I am not trying to recruit an army of leotard-wearing men—as cool as that would be—but instead asking for us all to give room for men (and women) to move beyond these suffocating boxes we have built around them. I want for men to not feel ashamed if they do like "girly" things, and I would also like for those things to not have to be referred to as "girly," but just as things.

From a young age, we instill a toxic idea of masculinity in our boys. We bar them from the princess dolls and the nail polish; we tell them to "be a man" to silence their tears. And we do this from an incredibly young age. Studies like this one debunking myths on boy's emotions, and this one on empathy differences between men and women have shown that as infants, boys and girls have equal abilities for empathy, but as they get older and social norms are thrusted upon them, boys don't cultivate their empathy and close relationships like girls do. The desire to be "manly" leads many boys feeling socially isolated, lonely and emotionally stoic. It can lead to future problems with relationships and difficulty coping with emotionally charged situations.

There is no one-fix solution, but we can start whittling away at the problem by opening the conversation on gender roles. Let us stop raising our boys and girls with rules that tell them they must act and present themselves in a certain way because of their birth certificate. When we see men being vulnerable and emotional, we should not dismiss them as weak. When we see political conversations talking about the potential emotional fragility of a female politician, we should question such assumptions and their sexist origins. I look forward to a day where masculinity and femininity can be seen as equally valid. A day when a man can have close same-sex friendships without his sexuality being questioned, where both men and women can express themselves emotionally, and where the Man Card is a thing of the past.

Viewpoint 

> *"Because masculinity is socially constructed, and one's status of manhood depends on the performance of several active traits, masculinity is both tenuous and elusive."*

Masculinity Is a Socially Constructed Set of Identities

Caleb P. Bay

In the following viewpoint, Caleb P. Bay argues that masculinity is hard to pin down, because it is a social construct. He reviews recent studies that link aggression to masculinity and demonstrate antigay and anti-women behaviors. He asks whether environmental stimuli contribute to toxic masculinity precisely because it is a social construct. Caleb P. Bay graduated from the University of Colorado, Boulder with a bachelor's degree in Psychology. He wrote his honor's thesis on "The Masculinity-Aggression Link."

"The Masculinity-Aggression Link: Increasing Aggressive Behavior through Priming Masculinity," by Caleb P. Bay, CU Scholar, 2017.

As you read, consider the following questions:

1. How does the author's citation of many studies advance his argument that masculinity is an artificial label?
2. How might environmental conditions make toxic masculinity inescapable?
3. What are the four previous movements in psychological theory of masculinity?

There is a great deal of conversation in mainstream media and in academia surrounding the pressures of womanhood. The Women's Marches that took place across the United States the day after President Trump's inauguration highlight the sexism toward and marginalization of women, transgender individuals, and others resulting from their gender (Women's March, 2017). In accordance with increasing public awareness of the matter, social scientists have long studied personal and institutional pressures on women. While the sexism experienced by women is incredibly important to understand, and while men occupy a privileged status in cultures like the United States, many researchers have begun to examine the ways in which manhood is also restricting and problematic. Indeed, Smiler (2004) asserts that feminist critiques of gender inspired the recent changes in psychological studies of masculinity.

Masculinity studies emphasizing the stress and "negatively lived experience of masculinity" emerged in the 1980s with scientists such as Pleck, who developed a sex role strain paradigm (Smiler, 2004, p. 19). Soon after, researchers in the deconstruction movement began to consider masculinity as the result of socialization and enculturation. Mosher and Tomkins (1988, p. 61) explain through script theory how individuals learn to be masculine through social teachings of how to act in a given situation, or "scene." The current movement in psychological theory of masculinity combines four previous movements to consider masculinity as a (1) socially constructed set of identities based in a (2) consistent underlying ideology defined in (3) opposition to the feminine that (4) produces strain on men as they construct their "own version of masculinity" through reference to "the masculine construct [that] is explicitly defined, and potentially altered, by the social setting" (Smiler, 2004, p. 21).

Current theories of masculinity allow for multiple types of masculinities. However, many studies continue to rely on the language of trait theory and identify key components that compose masculinity, or at least hegemonic masculinity (Connell & Messerschmidt, 2005). Through a review of several studies on male roles and traits, Brannon (1976, p. 20–23) consistently found the same few traits identified by a variety of researchers: a general opposition to the feminine, independence and risk-taking, emotional restriction/dysregulation, hyper-heterosexuality and anti-homosexuality, physical strength and competence, and aggression and dominance. Through the construction of the Auburn Differential Masculinity Inventory in a more contemporary study, Burk, Burkhart, and Sikorski (2004) identified the elements of hyper-masculinity to be the same as Brannon's findings from three decades earlier.

Because masculinity is socially constructed, and one's status of manhood depends on the performance of several active traits, masculinity is both tenuous and elusive. In an integral study to the psychological research on masculinity, Vandello, Bosson, Cohen, Burnaford, and Weaver (2008) found manhood, more than womanhood, to be considered a "precarious" state that must be earned and actively defended. Womanhood is also socially constructed, but Vandello and colleagues found that people generally see womanhood as passively obtained while manhood must be actively earned. In their experiments, threatening a man's masculinity provoked anxiety and activated physically aggressive thoughts. In subsequent projects, the researchers found that threatening one's manhood can actually lead to an increase in aggressive behavior (Bosson & Vandello, 2011; Bosson, Vandello, Burnaford, Weaver, & Wasti, 2009). Because aggression is such a

Guns and Masculinity

After the terrible mass shooting in Parkland, FL, debates about gun violence are on every TV, newspaper, and radio station. But with all this conversation, are we really getting to the heart of the matter? The fact is that 98% of mass shooters are male, and we too often neglect the link between toxic masculinity and gun violence.

From a young age, boys are taught to hide their emotions and negate parts of themselves. They learn that to "Be a Man" means to solve problems with dominance, aggression, and violence towards others (and even themselves). So much of our media tells us that guns are a symbol of masculine strength while the NRA appears to be running our country. All of this creates a culture where gun violence is normalized. Our children are dying—we as a society cannot afford to let this toxic narrative go unchallenged.

"Guns Are the Embodiment of Toxic Masculinity, Not the Solution," by Jennifer Siebel Newsom, The Representation Project, February 23, 2018.

core element of masculinity, aggressive displays are an effective tactic to reclaim one's manhood.

It is clear how inextricably linked aggression is to ideological masculinity when considering its connection to the other components of masculinity. For example, one study found that the intensity and frequency at which participants shocked an ostensible opponent was dependent on anger-proneness and whether their masculinity was threatened. However, for those who were prone to anger and received a threat to their masculinity, participants' level of restrictive emotionality (another key component of masculinity) predicted shock intensity and frequency such that those with more emotional restriction behaved more aggressively (Cohn, Jukupcak, Seibert, Hildebrandt, & Zeichner, 2010). Additionally, there is a large body of research that establishes a connection between masculine identification and antigay aggression and violence against women (Goodnight, Cook, Parrott, & Peterson, 2014; Vincent, Parrott, &

Peterson, 2011; Stotzer & Shih, 2012; Parrott & Zeichner, 2005; Parrott & Zeichner, 2003). Since heterosexuality and opposition to femininity are also key components of masculinity, men who strongly identify as masculine are more likely to exhibit antigay and antiwomen aggression.

Because aggression is so strongly linked with masculinity and many of its components, we predicted that it may not be necessary to actively threaten one's masculinity to increase aggressive behavior; and that instead, simply making the construct of masculinity accessible may result in increased accessibility of aggressive thoughts, and perhaps an increase in aggressive behavior. Bargh and Chartrand (1999) assert that the majority of our emotional and cognitive processing occurs on a non-conscious level in which our perceptions of our environment shape our behaviors and feelings without our awareness. Could environmental stimuli reflecting the construct of masculinity increase aggressive behavior simply by making masculine (and therefore aggressive) thoughts more accessible?

References

Bargh, J. A., & Chartrand, T. L. (1999). The unbearable automaticity of being. American psychologist, 54(7), 462.

Bosson, J. K., Vandello, J. A., Burnaford, R. M., Weaver, J. R., & Wasti, S. A. (2009). Precarious manhood and displays of physical aggression. Personality and Social Psychology Bulletin, 35(5), 623-634.

Bosson, J. K., & Vandello, J. A. (2011). Precarious manhood and its links to action and aggression. Current Directions in Psychological Science, 20(2), 82-86.

Brannon, Robert. The male sex role: Our culture's blueprint for manhood and what it's done for us lately. In Deborah David & Robert David (Eds.), The forty-nine percent majority: The male sex role (pp. 1-48). Reading, MA: Addison-Wesley.

Burk, L. R., Burkhart, B. R., & Sikorski, J. F. (2004). Construction and preliminary validation of the auburn differential masculinity inventory. Psychology of Men & Masculinity, 5(1), 4- 17.

Cohn, A. M., Jakupcak, M., Seibert, L. A., Hildebrandt, T. B., & Zeichner, A. (2010). The role of emotion dysregulation in the association between men's restrictive emotionality and use of physical aggression. Psychology of Men & Masculinity, 11(1), 53-64.

Conklin, John. (2013). Criminology (11th ed.). Boston, MA: Pearson.

Connell, R. W., & James Messerschmidt. (2005). Hegemonic Masculinity: Rethinking the Concept. Gender & Society, 19(6), 829-859.

Engelhardt, C. R., Bartholow, B. D., Kerr, G. T., & Goodnight, B. L., Cook, S. L., Parrott, D. J., & Peterson, J. L. (2014). Effects of masculinity, authoritarianism, and prejudice on antigay aggression: A path analysis of gender-role enforcement. Psychology of Men & Masculinity, 15(4), 437-444.

Mosher, Donald L. and Silvan S. Tomkins. (1988). Scripting the Macho Man: Hypermasculine Socialization and Enculturation. The Journal of Sex Research, 25(1), 60-84.

Parrott, D. J., & Zeichner, A. (2003). Effects of hypermasculinity on physical aggression against women. Psychology of Men & Masculinity, 4(1), 70-78.

Parrott, D. J., & Zeichner, A. (2005). Effects of sexual prejudice and anger on physical aggression toward gay and heterosexual men. Psychology of Men & Masculinity, 6(1), 3-17.

Smiler, A. P. (2004). Thirty years after the discovery of gender: Psychological concepts and measures of masculinity. Sex Roles, 50(1-2), 15-26.

Stotzer, R. L., & Shih, M. (2012). The relationship between masculinity and sexual prejudice in factors associated with violence against gay men. Psychology of Men & Masculinity, 13(2), 136-142.

Vandello, J. A., Bosson, J. K., Cohen, D., Burnaford, R. M., & Weaver, J. R. (2008). Precarious manhood. Journal of personality and social psychology, 95(6), 1325.

Vincent, W., Parrott, D. J., & Peterson, J. L. (2011). Effects of traditional gender role norms and religious fundamentalism on self-identified heterosexual men's attitudes, anger, and aggression toward gay men and lesbians. Psychology of Men & Masculinity, 12(4), 383-400.

VIEWPOINT 3

> *"Many of the characteristics that toxic masculinity prescribes in the twenty-first century, and those which contribute to the stigma surrounding men discussing their emotions and more seriously their mental health, can be traced back to the Victorian period."*

The Victorian Age Shaped Toxic Masculinity

Josephine Jobbins

In the following viewpoint, Josephine Jobbins argues that what we now call toxic masculinity had its roots in the nineteenth century during Queen Victoria's reign. Traits such as stoicism, strength, and athleticism became more important among men than did spirituality, for example. Physical strength, the author maintains, was necessary to fight and defend the British Empire. Josephine Jobbins is a School of History student at Queen Mary University of London. Among her academic interests is the history of women and gender, especially the women's movement.

"Man Up: The Victorian Origins of Toxic Masculinity," by Josephine Jobbins, QMUL School of History, 05/12/2017. https://projects.history.qmul.ac.uk/thehistorian/2017/05/12/man-up-the-victorian-origins-of-toxic-masculinity/.

As you read, consider the following questions:

1. What traits during Queen Victoria's reign in the British Empire became important among men?
2. According to this viewpoint, how is the culture of toxic masculinity described?
3. Why was athleticism important in the Victorian period?

The latest figures released by the Office for National Statistics (ONS) once again confirmed that men are three times more likely to commit suicide than women. Suicide remains the single biggest killer of men under the age of 45 in the UK. The lack of improvement in these figures has been combatted in recent years by specific campaigns, run by charities such as CALM, to challenge social stigmatisation of mental illness particularly for men, and offer support to those in crisis. The culture of toxic masculinity that modern society prescribes—one of a variety of models available to men—in which men have to be unemotional, strong, sexually dominant and violent, is clearly harmful to women and those in the LGBT+ community, but evidently it is also deeply damaging to men. In fact, it is literally killing them.

Damaging ideals of manhood, however, should not be understood as a purely modern phenomenon. Many of the characteristics that toxic masculinity prescribes in the twenty-first century, and those which contribute to the stigma surrounding men discussing their emotions and more seriously their mental health, can be traced back to the Victorian period. In the late nineteenth century, changing ideals of masculinity gave way to the dangerous expectations that still hold sway today.

Broadly, Victorian masculinity can be outlined as an ideology of spirituality and earnestness between 1837 and 1870, that changed to one of strength and stoicism from 1870. The ideas prevalent in the second half of this period can be understood as the foundations of a modern culture in which men are dying.

Masculinity, Male Privilege, and Intersectionality

All men are influenced by their upbringing, experience, and social environment which play a big role in determining one's view of masculinity and manhood. This means that masculinity is going to be different for everyone. Some particularly influential factors in shaping one's idea of manhood are **race, class, ability, sexual orientation, and gender**. Social justice advocates view these social identities as the most salient factors in society that determine who has power and privilege and who faces societal oppression. Men who are oppressed in one or more ways within this structure embody "**marginalized masculinities,**" which are ways of being men that are seen as less than or ridiculed by more privileged men as a means of constructing their own identities as men.

"Men and Masculinities," Colorado State University Women and Gender Advocacy Center.

Strength and athleticism were vital aspects of Victorian masculinity, as today. In the twenty-first century, this often takes the form of unrealistic expectations of the male body, as exemplified in the ever popular superhero film, which reflects a wider expectation of emotional strength. Physical strength in the Victorian era, however, took several forms. The first was the games-worshipping of the late nineteenth century. Between 1860 and 1880, games-playing was made compulsory in English public schools, where boys could demonstrate their physicality, and thus manliness, from an early age. In addition, manliness combined with religion in the phenomenon of muscular Christianity, commonly found in the writings of authors such as Charles Kingsley and Thomas Hughes. The hyper-masculinity of the late Victorian period was not at odds with other dominant cultural forces in the era.

Physical rigour was needed for men to be fit enough to fight and defend the British Empire. Late Victorian ideals of manhood as war-ready are evident in the literature of the time. To take one example, Rudyard Kipling's poem 'If...' (1895), which acts as a guide to manhood for his son, takes inspiration from colonial administrator Leander Starr Jameson, presenting him as the ideal man. One characteristic which the poem promotes is that of level-headedness or stoicism suggested, for example, in the first two lines: 'If you can keep your head when all about you/ Are losing theirs and blaming it on you'. Although imperialism is of little significance today, ideas of stoicism still endure. It is a widely held notion that boys don't cry and men are often depicted as rational and unemotional. And it is this set of beliefs which undoubtedly contributes to the higher rate of suicide among men today.

It is interesting to consider the motivation behind the cultural ideals surrounding masculinity, specifically whether the promotion of strength, virility and stoicism were, and are, in reaction to new ideas about the place and position of women in society. Both the late nineteenth century and the twenty-first century have seen the promotion of greater equality for women and the challenging of traditional gender roles. In the late Victorian era, this manifested itself in the so-called flight from domesticity, which saw men delaying marriage or not marrying at all, and often vehement anti-suffrage campaigns.

2017 has already witnessed women passionately campaigning in the global Women's March in January, and on International Women's Day in March; perhaps the toxic masculinity that prescribes such damaging ideals to men is a reaction. Men have only recently begun to be studied as gendered beings within history and it is clear it is important to continue to scrutinise cultural expectation of masculinity in the modern day.

Viewpoint 4

> *"Ultimately, there is no necessary physiological reason for holding that unruly or rebellious behavior has to accompany endocrine changes in the teen years."*

Wealthy White Boys Are Allowed to Be Toxic

Ashwini Tambe

In the following viewpoint, Ashwini Tambe argues that pegging adolescence as a phase of irresponsible behavior is a relatively new phenomenon. Often rationalized as "boys will be boys," she examines the term "adolescence" and its association with rebellion. She also addresses the double standard between what is allowable for wealthy white boys and not allowable for other boys. Ashwini Tambe is an Associate Professor of Women's Studies at the University of Maryland. She also serves as the Editorial Director of Feminist Studies, an academic journal for feminist scholarship.

As you read, consider the following questions:

1. Does the phrase "boys will be boys" excuse toxic behavior?
2. What are the expectations of adolescent boys?
3. According to this viewpoint, why are the actions of white wealthy boys condoned?

Supreme Court nominee Brett Kavanaugh's actions as a 17- and 18-year-old are at the center of a public firestorm.

"I've been really troubled by the excuse offered by too many that this was a high school incident, and 'boys will be boys,' said Sen. Chris Coons during testimony by Christine Blasey Ford before the Senate Judiciary Committee on Sept. 27.

But Trump surrogates such as Kellyanne Conway have dismissed his actions are merely those of a "teenager." The adult Kavanaugh cannot be held accountable, such logic goes, for these alleged youthful indiscretions.

What exactly do we mean by teenage behavior? And who gets to be this kind of teenager?

In the United States, the teen years are frequently assumed to be a time of experimentation, risk-taking and rebellion. But this notion of adolescence as a phase of irresponsible behavior is a relatively new invention.

The Idea of Adolescence: A History

It was only in the first decade of the 20th century that U.S. psychologists came up with the idea of a separate life phase called adolescence and began treating these years as an extension of childhood.

The term "adolescence"—emerging from the Latin word for youth, adulescence—had circulated in English since the Middle Ages, but modern psychologists carved it out as a chronologically specific phase during which a person prepared for adulthood while legally remaining a child. And, as my research shows, U.S. psychologists' idea of adolescence took time to take root and traveled slowly to other parts of the world, even encountering resistance in places such as India.

In the U.S., compulsory schooling and age-based classrooms inaugurated in the 1870s laid the groundwork for imagining teen years as a sheltered phase. By the 1910s, educators came to a consensus that compulsory high school should extend until age

18. Before then, most men and women under that age could be, and were, expected to work, get married and even have children.

The most forceful explanation of adolescence as a distinct phase appeared in the work of G. Stanley Hall, founder of the *American Journal of Psychology* and the first president of the American Psychological Association. His 1904 "Adolescence" described a phase that spread out between the ages of 12 and 18, encompassing the breaking of voice and facial hair for boys and the first menstrual period and breast development for girls—and the emotional maturation following these physical developments.

While the end of childhood had been marked in many cultures with a rite of passage at puberty—such as the bar mitzvah or the quinceanera—he proposed that the emotional transition actually lasted longer and ended later.

Rebelliousness

Hall described adolescence as a period of rebelliousness and individualism. Rebelliousness, he believed, was a developmental requirement for the full flowering of self. He also expressed anxiety around how to manage boys' sexual impulses during the teen years, devoting an entire chapter to the "dangers" of sexual development. More than any other psychologist, Hall contributed to the understanding of adolescence as a time of heightened storm and stress and emotional turbulence. His chosen constellation of features—rebelliousness, emotional turbulence, sexual recklessness—became the blueprint for analyzing and assessing the problems of young people.

But here's the catch. Many of these early descriptions of adolescence were written for and about boys of the same social background as the author—white and middle-class. It was primarily such boys who could enjoy an extended childhood characterized by social and sexual experimentation. Lower-class boys and most black boys were expected to grow up earlier by entering the manual labor market and assuming responsibilities in their teens.

Toxic Masculinity and the Suppression of Trauma

Research indicates that one in six men experienced sexual abuse at some point during their childhood, and this is probably a low estimate, as it doesn't account for non-contact experiences, which can also have lasting effects.

In addition, when thinking about the statistic, we need to acknowledge the barriers that may prevent a man from disclosing his experiences; not only is there a lack of awareness about the issue and its prevalence (I often hear men say that they thought they were "the only one"), but societal expectations about what it means to "be a man" may cause a survivor to suppress his trauma.

From an early age, men receive the message that they should never be, or even appear, vulnerable or weak; the idea that men cannot be victims is central to gender socialization. The reality is that men can and do experience all forms of violence, including sexual abuse and sexual assault. Unfortunately, due to the barriers outlined above (as well as other barriers, like lack of access to resources), most men who have had such experiences do not begin to address the negative effects until their late 30s or 40s, if ever.

"Millions of Men Suffer in Silence After Sexual Abuse. How Can We Help Them Better?" by David Lisak, Guardian News and Media Limited, November 25, 2017.

A prolonged preparation for adulthood was actually available only to those with economic means.

Double Standards

A similar double standard is echoed today in the way Kavanaugh's supporters grant him leeway. Sympathetic accounts contextualize Kavanaugh's behavior as part of boys' culture at the elite institutions where he studied and just "rough horseplay." This reaction is part of a social tendency to see wealthy white boys' actions as innocently naughty, rather than dangerous. Black boys, on the other hand, routinely experience "adultification," as historian Ann Ferguson called it—the assignment of adult motivations and ability. We do not need to look far for contemporary examples: Trayvon Martin, age 17, was stalked and killed by a vigilante neighbor who suspected he was a threat. Even 12-year-old Tamir Rice was killed because police officers thought he was a danger. And 17-year-old boys of color are regularly tried as adults and sent to prison.

What About Adolescent Girls?

Expectations for teenage behavior are also deeply gendered in the United States.

Innocently naughty behavior has historically been the prerogative of teenage boys rather than girls. Rebelliousness was frowned upon if girls—whether black or white—expressed it. Historian Crista DeLuzio goes so far as to depict much of the early writing on adolescence as "boyology." Girls were simply not imagined, in psychologists' work, to have the same entitlement to experimentation and innocent risk-taking.

This double standard continues to permeate U.S. culture. There is a telling relevant example from the U.S. college context: Sororities, unlike fraternities, are bound by a ban on alcohol by the National Panhellenic Conference.

Kavanaugh's alleged actions as a teen under the influence of alcohol have not tainted his reputation as a judge for many on the political right. But Christine Blasey Ford and Deborah Ramirez are pilloried by Donald Trump as unreliable because they were possibly drunk at age 15 and 18. Kavanaugh's own views on teenage girls' accountability are telling: In a controversial decision he offered as a federal judge, he called to delay a 17-year-old pregnant undocumented girl's access to an abortion. Although he claimed it was because she was a minor and needed parental consent, his delay could have forced the 17-year-old into motherhood—an adult consequence.

Social Expectations

Humans going through puberty certainly experience endocrine changes and neural growth. But our social expectations for behavior are what permit—and indeed elicit—specific types of acts, such as drunken unruliness. As psychologist Jeffrey Arnett notes, Hall's ideas about adolescent storm and stress have been widely repudiated by subsequent generations of psychologists, even if some of the physiological changes he tracked are still considered accurate. And Crista de Luzio notes that in the 17th century, youth was experienced as a "relatively smooth" period in New England Puritan culture in contrast to Europe in the same era. Widespread youthful rebelliousness, she argues, corresponded more generally with social instability.

Ultimately, there is no necessary physiological reason for holding that unruly or rebellious behavior has to accompany endocrine changes in the teen years. Our uneven expectations about teenage behavior—condoning white wealthy boys' actions but not those of girls or other boys—say more, then, about us than about teens themselves.

VIEWPOINT 5

"[Teachers] are used to seeing boys get involved in science activities, while girls sit to the side of the lab and chat, not encouraged to take part."

Teachers Influence Gender Equality

Fatma Özdemir Uluç

In the following viewpoint, Fatma Özdemir Uluç argues that each child has the right to develop his or her full potential irrespective of gender. Within a school system, teachers may inadvertently reinforce gender inequality by the way they talk to and behave with their students. They may have their own gender biases, too. Approaches to sports become particular problematic. Fatma Özdemir Uluç is an education expert based in Turkey. She served as team leader of the European Union–funded study, "Promoting Gender Equality in Education," for the British Council in Turkish schools from 2014 to 2016.

As you read, consider the following questions:

1. How might teachers reinforce gender equality? Inequality?
2. What games are used with children to create an understanding of gender equality?
3. Why are schools the right entry point to have discussions about gender equality?

"How to Approach Teaching Gender Equality to Boys and Girls," by Fatma Özdemir Uluç, British Council, February 23, 2017. Reprinted by permission.

What's the most effective way to talk to adults about gender equality?

We start by talking to them about children. Our main argument is that every child has a right to reach their full potential, and gender inequality prevents this by limiting what they can and can't do. Once we explain that that's why we have to do things differently, then the conversation becomes more open and interesting.

Second, we show how people unconsciously reinforce gender roles. Normally, teachers will protest that they treat both sexes the same. Our challenge is to make them aware that they often behave differently towards boys and girls—perhaps without realising it—and reveal how this behaviour affects their students.

How do you start the conversation?

We asked teachers what they called the children they teach in nursery and primary schools, and found out that boys are commonly referred to as 'my son' while girls are often 'my beautiful daughter'. These are used as general terms of endearment for all young children in southern Turkey (an equivalent would be people calling boys 'son' or 'sport', and girls 'sweetie' or 'my angel'), but unwittingly, it also forms clear ideas in the children's heads that they are distinct from each other because of their gender. Adults often use language and adjectives that link very strongly to gender bias.

We also asked teachers how they select students for after-school activities, and found that children are encouraged to choose clubs that 'fit' their gender. Almost all the girls would choose fashion club, and the boys would end up at a plane-making class, or something similar. The child's choice would be heavily influenced by teachers and parents.

I experienced this myself, when my four-year-old daughter came home from pre-school and said, 'Mum, girls cannot play basketball, right?' Even at this young age, she had this impression—and she was checking with me. We want all boys and girls to be given a chance to try everything. That way, they can work out what they enjoy.

We look through the teachers' textbooks with them to find examples of gender bias. We found this exercise to be the most helpful way for teachers to understand what gender equality is. In one third-grade textbook, we found a picture of a family doing the house chores together, which looked very positive at first. But when we looked at the speech bubbles attached to the family, the other family members are all looking to the mother to lead: the father is asking what he should do next, and the boy is looking for approval from his mother. So in a subtle way, women are still shown as responsible for household chores.

Do all teaching materials need to be updated as gender-neutral?

Updated books would help to improve the understanding of gender equality in schools. But even if the content of the textbooks does not change, teachers can still point these examples out as examples of gender inequality. This encourages children to think much more critically about the content they read, which is even more important.

What specific exercises can teachers do with children?

We developed a card game where you can match female and male figures doing the same profession, such as doctors and scientists. We adapted this for pre-school children as a colouring exercise, where they can colour the matching cards.

Remember 'snakes and ladders'? Well, we imagined this as a gender game. Children are given statements related to gender: either positive messages, such as 'everyone has a right to education', 'it is up to us to treat everyone equally', and 'everyone can do household chores'; or negative messages like 'it is more important for boys to go to school', 'male students are lazier', and 'girls and boys cannot play the same games together'.

The children either move forwards up the ladders or backwards down the snakes—depending on whether they agree or disagree with each statement. The aim is to replace negative messages with positive ones, so children who find themselves at the top of a snake have the chance to change the negative message into a positive one. If they do, they get to roll the dice for another turn. This game was particularly popular.

How do you approach this with older students?

We also worked with high-school students, who responded really positively to the exercises we gave them. For example, in literature classes, we introduced an activity on proverbs and idioms, which are extremely well-loved and popular in Turkey. We found many examples of gender bias in Turkish proverbs such as 'a boy grows up to be strong, a girl grows up to be nothing', 'if they say there is a wedding in the sky, women would try to build a ladder', and 'it is the female bird that builds the nest'. We talked about where these perceptions on men and women's roles in society came from, sometimes rewriting them to be more neutral and progressive.

We also rewrote some popular stories and fairy tales. One school we worked with put on a play about Cinderella, casting a boy in the lead role to find out how this changed the story. We talked about the importance of girls and boys having lots of different options in life. Not every girl has to wait for a prince to save her.

Sports are also important. You can very easily see the discrimination here between boys and girls in the options available to them. Boys can play football, but it is very rare to see a girls' team. Even basketball is seen as a boy's sport, so as part of the project, we helped set up girls' football and basketball teams to give the students choices. We also built mixed teams, so everyone could play together—often for the first time.

Why is teaching gender equality important in Turkey?

Turkish school textbooks don't have a single woman visualised or mentioned in the text as a politician. How can you expect to have women represented equally in parliament, when girls are never told that that is an option for them? We have policies about gender equality in writing, and legislation more or less in line with international commitments—but there is still no change.

Turkish women have had the vote since 1934 and have the same legal rights as men, but they remain far from equal. In fact, even the term gender equality is divisive in Turkey. The government prefers the term 'gender fairness' to reflect its views that women and men are not 'truly equal'. More than half (60 per cent) of Turkish young women do not complete upper-secondary education, and Turkey ranked 131st out of 145 countries in the World Economic Forum's gender equality index.

What was it like talking to schools and teachers in Turkey about gender?

The whole issue of gender equality is very new in Turkey, and our target audiences were in remote, rural and conservative areas. Education staff were afraid to do something which might cause controversy, and were not even aware of Turkey's international commitments on gender equality. Turkey was an early adopter of these commitments, but the UN has criticised the extent to which they have been implemented.

So, first we had to have a discussion about exactly what we meant by this term in an educational context, and why it is so important for Turkish society. We explained that when women work outside the home, it boosts the economy (Turkey wants to be a top ten economy by 2023, the centenary of the Turkish republic). We also discussed Turkey's worrying rate of violence against women, and how this damages families and communities. Once you create a common understanding of what gender equality means, then you can get people on board.

What training already exists for teachers?

Most teachers have had no training in gender issues in education. This is the way they've grown up and always lived, so they don't see any problem when, at school, girls clean the classrooms and boys play sport outside. They are used to seeing boys get involved in science activities, while girls sit to the side of the lab and chat, not encouraged to take part. For teachers in many parts of Turkey, this is not disturbing at all. It is normal—and this is why training them is so important.

If there is no equality standard in your private or professional life, it's very hard to understand that there even is an issue. So at first, we experienced resistance. People were confused about what we were trying to do—whether it was about feminism, or lesbian, gay, bisexual and transgender (LGBT) issues. They were not sure what 'gender' meant, so the 'equality' part was hard to explain at first. Once this was clear, teachers could appreciate why it was important.

Teachers and teacher trainers need to understand gender issues, get rid of their prejudices and realise why they should not transmit these to their students. Three or five days of training is a good start, but the subject of gender should form a central part of teacher training before they go into the classroom.

How can we encourage parents to reinforce gender equality at home?

Our main dispute at the start of the project was the role that parents should play. The Turkish education ministry suggested that we should target parents, rather than teachers: it might be too late to focus on gender equality once children have started school at age six, as their attitudes would already be shaped by their families.

But we wanted to work the other way round. We knew that if we targeted schools, the students could pass on the messages to their parents. That is why we always included parents' meetings and training sessions in our campaign, although again, we faced

Redefining Masculinity

Hypermasculinity—also known as toxic masculinity—describes the narrow ideas about what it means to "be a man." It's the exaggeration of male stereotypical behaviours like an emphasis on physical strength, aggression and sexuality. It is also the idea that men and boys shouldn't show their emotions, talk about their feelings or show vulnerability.

Teach About Healthy Relationships and Emotional Regulation

One of the main features of hypermasculinity is the use of violence to solve problems. Media is rife with examples of tough, angry men using their muscles—not their relational skills—to deal with conflict. Encouraging boys' emotional vocabularies and teaching them assertive communication and anger management skills will help to nurture healthier individuals and relationships.

Challenge Toxic Masculinity

Learn what it is and why it's a problem. Point it out in media, advertising and sports culture. Speak up if you hear language that contributes to a culture of toxic masculinity and violence. You are your child's biggest influence, make sure it's a good one.

"Redefining Masculinity: Tips for Raising Healthy Kids in a Hypermasculinized World," YWCA Metro Vancouver.

many challenges. Depending on the province, either the mothers or the fathers came to the meeting, but never together. In Urfa in south-eastern Turkey, for example, almost all our participants were men. And once we were working with secondary-school-aged students, it became almost impossible to bring either parent into the fold.

Here's an example. One of our social science teachers set homework asking students to observe their family for a week, and find out who was getting the most tired. A sixth-grade boy reported back that his older sister and his mother were the most tired, because they were doing everything in the house: preparing the food and doing all the chores. Even though his older sister was preparing for her university exam, she was doing all the work – even down to bringing him his tea. The teacher decided to have a parents' evening and carefully discuss ways to treat boys and girls equally. Families are crucial, but to break this vicious circle, schools are the right entry point, through which to raise questions.

Boys also face harmful stereotypes. How can we support boys?

This was an important part of our project. The Turkish education ministry is sceptical about feminism, and thought at first we wanted to ignore boys. We explained that gender inequality is not just about women and girls. It also negatively affects men and boys.

We told them about the link between gender bias and violent behaviour in boys, especially violence against women. This is sadly a significant problem in Turkish society. Domestic violence is related to culturally supported attitudes about who should be in control in a relationship. When we were able to demonstrate the clear societal consequences of the current gender imbalance, the ministry fully embraced the project.

Teachers were also surprised by what our research revealed about their behaviour towards boys in the classroom. For example, boys said that teachers had a no-tolerance attitude to their 'bad' behaviour, while when the girls acted in the same way the teachers did not react at all. The boys felt that they picked up the labels of being 'naughty' and 'useless' quickly and easily, making them feeling side-lined and neglected. We need to focus on boys just as much as girls, and make sure that no one feels left out or favoured.

> *"We can decide what stories to tell and what stories to live by, what principles to claim, and what habits to release. It's a powerful claim, and the first step in changing the narrative around the misuse of power and oppressive systems of domination."*

Open Communication Can Change the Narrative of Toxic Masculinity

Madeline Schaefer

In the following viewpoint, Madeline Schaefer argues that conversations are necessary to identify and realize positive masculinity in all of its forms. As evidence, she points to a recent American Friends Service Committee conference and presents five key takeaways. These include oppressive masculinity as the root of violence and war. She also emphasizes the importance of open communication for healing and large-scale change from the effects of oppressive masculinity. Madeline Schaefer is the Friends Relations Associate for the American Friends Service Committee, a Quaker organization, in Philadelphia, Pennsylvania.

"What Does Healthy Masculinity Look Like?" by Madeline Schaefer, American Friends Service Committee, February 6, 2014. Reprinted by permission.

As you read, consider the following questions:

1. What is the relationship between healing from negative effects of masculinity and peace-building?
2. What are the five takeaways from the American Friends Service Committee's conference?
3. How is oppressive masculinity the root of violence and war?

At a recent conference held by the American Friends Service committee, I picked up a piece of literature titled "Principles of a Noble Man."

A noble man, it says, is a man of his word. He has a sense of responsibility for his own well-being and that of others in his circle. He rejects any form of abuse, is sensitive and understanding, takes time to reflect, pray, and include ceremony in his life. The principles of a noble man, I thought, are principles of a noble woman. They are principles of a noble human.

Those principles were being distributed by the National Compadres Network, one of the organizations represented at that conference, held back in December. Nearly 50 people gathered at Friends Center, AFSC's central office, to think together about "Masculinity, Healing, and Peacebuilding."

How can harmful patriarchal definitions of manhood be transformed so that they are more diverse, more authentic, more whole?

This topic is, for many, new and uncharted territory—rarely do we have conversations about the positive role that masculinity might play in creating a more peaceful world. But there is so much to be discussed that has been unexamined, and this conference created the opportunity for a wide-ranging, rich conversation.

Participants included AFSC staff, scholars, storytellers, community organizers, youth, and teachers. It was a unique mixture of people, of experiences, of communication styles; but everyone involved seemed committed to bringing their full selves in a spirit of respect and authenticity.

Together they searched for a positive and active construction of masculinity while examining its harmful legacy as understood, in part, through the hurt, healing, and stories from conference participants. I had been generously invited to observe the second and final day of the conference—a taste.

The first day had been a series of small breakout sessions on topics such as "Is masculinity a social construct?" and "Men as healers and peace-builders." The discussions that had taken place during those sessions had created a strong sense of intimacy; a connection that was palpable on what was only the second day.

As a woman simply observing the day of dialogue reflecting on the breakout sessions the day before, I could tell that I was listening to something unique, something raw and new and charged with energy.

One woman shared how hearing the stories of the ways that dominant models of masculinity had hurt many of the men at the conference inspired her to look anew on her interactions with her grandsons. I was also powerfully reminded of the negative impact that systems of violence and oppression have on all of us, of every race and gender. Working for peace requires that we all come to the table, examine our own hurts, listen to the suffering of others, understand the legacy of oppression, and then work together to change the structures that keep each one of us from being fully human.

Again and again it was emphasized that we all are telling the story of masculinity right now—in the relationships we build, the media we consume, the values we choose to adopt. We can decide what stories to tell and what stories to live by, what principles to claim, and what habits to release. It's a powerful claim, and the first step in changing the narrative around the misuse of power and oppressive systems of domination.

Below is a list of "takeaways" from one of the conference's organizers and AFSC's Assistant General Secretary for Integration and Impact, Renata Fletcher.

Oppressive Masculinity Is a Root of War and Violence of All Types.

The narrow and destructive construct of masculinity we seek to change is rooted in centuries-old supremacy, patriarchy, and oppression played out through events such as slavery, colonization, and war. Massacres, stolen people, stolen land, and persistent attempts to marginalize or even destroy groups of people across the world and their cultures have multi-generational impact and have created legacies of hurt and pain. It continues to be used to control and conquer.

Positive Masculinity Is Constructed from Not One but Multiple Definitions, Identities, and Self and External Concepts.

All of these masculinities must be acknowledged, honored, respected, and present in healing and peace-building as men.

As Individuals, We Must Prioritize Our Own Healing Where Hurt and Wounds Are Present.

We cannot be fully effective in our lives and work if we ourselves are tired, sick, and unhealed. (As one participant put it, "we can't be sick healers.")

The Strength of Our Individual and Collective Efforts Must Be Rooted in Our Stories, and in Telling and Sharing Those Stories.

Through these stories, we are able to heal and also to fully acknowledge each other's dignity and humanity, including how we have done harm both to ourselves and others. The work, approaches, and methods of the majority of people in the room were rooted in stories. One academic participant talked of his activism to push researchers to "put a human face" to all of their work and to everything they do.

A Strong and Effective Community of Healing and Peace-Building Is Wholly Reliant on Individual Healing Taking Place, As Well As on the Power of Relationships Between People, Communities, and Organizations.

We must support each other lovingly in our work and lives together. The power of relationships is so strong, and those active in various aspects of the wider social movement must broaden how we support each other. It is narrow definitions that keep us from one another and from realizing larger scale change for our communities. We need each other—as individuals, as organizations, as sectors.

Formal and informal institutions and systems may be most effectively transformed from the inside out.

Periodical and Internet Sources Bibliography

The following articles have been selected to supplement the diverse views presented in this chapter.

Avmo Amin, Anna Kågesten, Emmanuel Adebayo, and Ventrakamen Chandra-Mouli, "Addressing Gender Socialization and Masculinity Norms Among Adolescent Boys: Policy and Programmatic Implications, *Journal of Adolescent Health*, March 2018, https://www.ncbi.nlm.nih.gov/pmc/articles/PMC5817048/.

Brown University, "Unlearning Toxic Masculinity," n.d., https://www.brown.edu/campus-life/health/services/promotion/general-health-social-wellbeing-sexual-assault-dating-violence-get-involved-prevention/unlearning.

"Changing Harmful Gender Norms," Unilever, n.d., https://www.unilever.com/sustainable-living/enhancing-livelihoods/opportunities-for-women/Challenging-harmful-gender-norms/.

Dom, "Is Masculinity a Social Construct?" MindCoolness, February 26, 2018, https://www.mindcoolness.com/blog/is-masculinity-a-social-construct/.

Chris Ferguson, "Is a New 'Masculinity' Program at UT Wrong About Men? [Commentary]," *Houston Chronicle*, May 10, 2018, https://www.houstonchronicle.com/local/gray-matters/article/university-of-texas-program-toxic-masculinity-12901478.php.

Caroline Crosson Gilpin and Natalie Proulx, "Boys to Men: Teaching about Masculinity in an Age of Change," The New York Times, April 12, 2018, https://www.nytimes.com/2018/04/12/learning/lesson-plans/boys-to-men-teaching-and-learning-about-masculinity-in-an-age-of-change.html.

Katie Groves, "Men for Social Change Strive to Educate, Change Social Norms," *Daily Evergreen*, January 29, 2018, https://dailyevergreen.com/25457/life/men-for-social-change-strive-to-educate-change-social-norms/.

Hannah Meeske, "Masculinity as a Social Construction," *Odyssey*, July 26, 2016, https://www.theodysseyonline.com/masculinity-as-social-construction.

"New Promundo Report Explores the Links Between Harmful Masculine Norms and 8 Forms of Violence," May 4, 2018, https://promundoglobal.org/2018/05/04/report-links-harmful-masculine-norms-violence/.

Orpheus Sen, "How a World That Glorifies Masculinity Ultimately Creates Inequality, YKA Media, https://www.youthkiawaaz.com/2017/04/an-account-of-a-misogynist-world-the-battle-between-patriarchy-and-feminism-2/.

James Sitzmann, "Is Femininity and Masculinity a Social or Biological Construct?" *Medium*, September 28, 2016, https://medium.com/@eccentric_eddy/is-femininity-and-masculinity-a-social-or-biological-construct-62b21028455f.

Ruth C. White, "Is Toxic Masculinity a Mask for Anxiety?" OpenDemocracy, March 22, 2018, https://www.opendemocracy.net/transformation/ruth-c-white/is-toxic-masculinity-mask-for-anxiety.

CHAPTER 3

Is It Necessary for Males to Demonstrate Aggression?

Chapter Preface

In the aftermath of mass shootings, politicians and journalists are turning to psychologists and other experts to find out more about the men who perpetrate these acts of violence. They question linkages between the violence and mental illness. Viewpoints examine existing studies and data and either confirm or refute the linkage depending on how they interpret the data. Although the connection to mental illness may not be present, there can be a correlation between acts of domestic violence and abuse and mass violence. To answer the question of the necessity for males to show aggression, in the case of these mass shooters, a response is they have a history of it. Contributing factors include the social environment.

But most acts of toxic masculinity do not result in mass violence. Some viewpoints insist that lessons of toxic behavior begin in adolescence when demonstrations of emotion and intellect are shunned in favor of violence and aggression. If boys do not exhibit the "right" male behaviors, they open themselves up to scrutiny, shame, and bullying.

Viewpoints argue that men need to learn how to express themselves and seek help. If men are the victims of rape, for example, staying silent may only result in more serious issues including depression and suicide. Men should have a choice in how they present themselves. In a particularly moving narrative, an eight-year-old boy feels accomplished when he intentionally hits another softball player with his ball, earning the recognition of this teammates. Later at a fast food restaurant, he opts for the fairy in the kid's meal, although the server tucks in a toy car believing the child has made the wrong choice.

The following chapter presents perspectives of boys and men and the ramifications of exposure to and living with toxic masculinity, sometimes with disastrous results.

Viewpoint 1

> *"Rather than enacting an aberrant tangent, Whitman's first murders fulfilled—in the most extreme way—the code of mid-century American masculinity he had absorbed, practiced, and even struggled against, defining real men as dominant and powerful and real women as subordinate and submissive."*

Toxic Masculinity Is Responsible for Domestic Violence and Mass Shootings

Jo Scott-Coe

In the following excerpted viewpoint, Jo Scott-Coe argues that true-crime narratives tend to deflect serious examination of the misogynistic attitudes, abuse, and/or fatal violence that often precede a public massacre. The author analyzes writings of 1966 UT Austin sniper Charles Whitman and his wife, Kathy Leissner, to emphasize how inflexible gender attitudes and judgments took a profoundly toxic and eventually fatal toll in private, long before Whitman's display of hyper-masculine force from atop a landmark tower. Jo Scott-Coe is the author of two nonfiction books as well as pieces in such publications as The Los Angeles Times and Best American Essays.

"Invisible Women, Fairy Tale Death: How Stories of Public Murder Minimize Terror at Home," by Jo Scott-Coe, *American Studies Journal* 62 (2017). http://www.asjournal.org/62-2017/invisible-women-fairy-tale-death-stories-public-murder-minimize-terror-home/

As you read, consider the following questions:

1. What does it mean that one of the sniper's peers reportedly said "If Charlie was a monster, then so are we all"?
2. How did Whitman put his wife on a pedestal, according to the author?
3. How does failing to examine domestic abuse by mass shooters ultimately harm women?

Four years ago, in an essay titled "Shooting Sprees Start with Women," I explored how the private brutality that precedes violent spectacle is often buried by coverage of the public event. An accumulation of such stories—from Sandy Hook to Orlando, from Casper College to UCLA—still treats domestic death or wounding as an afterthought to more serious or offensive crimes.

As a result, those terrorized in private do not fully register on the compass of collective outrage, except as targets of direct or indirect blame for the public outcome. In 2015, Bill Maher argued on his show *Real Time* that young males commit mass killings because they simply can't "get laid," even though commercials depict women as ready and willing sexual objects (n. pag.). Maher didn't mention to his applauding audience that a significant percentage of these same men stalk, abuse, or kill women as a prelude to attacking strangers (Everytown 2–5). Furthermore, Maher's commentary unwittingly replicated the entitled misogynist "reasoning" often broadcast by the killers themselves (Schonfeld)—as in the cases of Marc Lepine (1989), George Hennard (1991), George Sodini (2009), and Elliot Rodger (2014).

One enduring example shows how ingrained our current script and its gendered erasures can be. Since 1966, writers, artists, and documentarians have retold the story of Charles Whitman's clock tower rampage at the University of Texas at Austin, which left nearly fifty people dead or wounded, including Whitman himself. Unlike most mass killers, he was married rather than single. But like many others, he murdered women at home—his mother, Margaret, and his wife, Kathleen—before shooting anyone else. And like many men who commit similar attacks, Whitman viewed women as objects both to desire and control.

It is important to examine how the UT Austin narrative—like so many others—diminishes, romanticizes, or sequesters domestic murder. I will argue that this repeating dynamic reflects something all too ordinary and self-implicating: fear and suspicion of women. Whitman's actions and personal writings must be understood within this context. Newly available primary documents finally make it possible to consider the perspective of his wife as well as her family.

Charles Whitman's 1966 Rampage

The UT rampage was not the first mass murder in American history, but it was the first televised shooting of its kind, and the sensational scale of Whitman's crimes generated media headlines across the country. [...] Story after story addresses Whitman's Eagle Scout achievement, his military training, drug use, fascination with guns, hatred of his father as well as his much-debated brain tumor (Ward). Limited attention has been paid to Whitman's attitudes about women and sex. Whitman's wife and mother are usually rendered through romantic/sensational re-enactments or minimalism/omission, all in service of "true crime" formula with its victims, heroes, and obvious villain. This repeated and recursive glossing suggests gendered habits of mind—both of authors and audiences—rather than direct intention or malice.

As a former Boy Scout and altar boy, as a handsome, white college student and former Marine, Whitman embodied the mid-century, postwar "All-American guy." Yet privileges of gender and race, bound with the motifs of American individualism, have cast Whitman as a "crazy, deranged individual who had suddenly gone completely berserk"—an exception to the rule (Special Report of the Grand Jury 1, par. 2). In his book, *Murder over a Girl*, Ken Corbett describes gendered inattention this way: "One of the ways that [boys] get to be boys is that they get to be invisible," meaning, in part, that classmates, colleagues, family, and friends "refuse to know what they knew" (151). In a similar vein, one of Whitman's peers recounted his pranks and other high-risk behaviors after the massacre with amusement and disbelief, saying: "If Charlie was a monster, then so are we all" (qtd. in Dugger 3).

There's yet another factor which has camouflaged Whitman's attitudes. In contrast with "lone-wolf" shooters who left behind over-the-top diatribes against women, Whitman's surviving letters and journals rely heavily on the language of idealization. Yet his attitudes are no less objectifying, despite his repetition of "love" and other flowery terms. Furthermore, his idealization divides women into simultaneous targets of worship and punishment (Madonna/whore), demonstrating what Julia Kristeva calls a "conjunction of opposites (courtliness and sadism)" (162–63). Rather than enacting an aberrant tangent, Whitman's first murders fulfilled—in the most extreme way—the code of mid-century American masculinity he had absorbed, practiced, and even struggled against, defining real men as dominant and powerful and real women as subordinate and submissive. The pattern normalizes victimization of women when individual men do not see themselves living up to the stereotype of their own gender: "The target must already be seen as legitimate [...]. [M]asculinity may not be the experience of power. But it is the experience of entitlement to power" (Kimmel 181, 185).

Violence against woman can thus embody a primal, "restorative" strike to (re)assert masculine dominance, "returning [...] to the moment before that sense of vulnerability and dependency was felt" (Kimmel 177–78). Historian Gerda Lerner hypothesized that the awe-inspiring power of women was first venerated and then objectified, reflecting male dread, envy, and eventually ownership of the capacity to create and sustain life (45–53). In this way, Whitman's first murders can be understood as acts of self-ordination to "divine" male dominion over life and death—first in private, then from more than 300 feet above sidewalks and streets. It is no coincidence that his first target from the tower was a heavily pregnant woman, Claire Wilson, whose child was aborted in utero with his first bullet (Maitland). Confronted by repeated failures as a Marine, as a college engineering student, and as a husband, Whitman still felt entitled by a toxic residue of privileges he was born into as a white male Southerner. Storytelling that avoids (or "abjects") gender, sexuality, or race inadvertently re-inscribes that same toxic inheritance.

In addition to the investigative documents assembled by law enforcement agencies, a significant sample of Whitman's personal writing (from ages 15 to 25) was publicly preserved and is now housed in the Austin History Center. Documents in this archive include notebooks, a day planner from his first year of college, a diary, miscellaneous "inspirational" notes, and four letters he composed within hours of the shooting. This was the extent of the accessible record until 2015, when I was granted exclusive access to additional materials from the private collection maintained by his wife's eldest brother.

[...]

A Fractured Fairy Tale: Whitman as "Man"—Kathy as "Wife"

We can now read Whitman's attitudes by tracing them forward in select letters to Kathy beginning two months prior to their marriage. An even larger sample of her letters—both to Whitman and her own mother—provide insightful points of comparison, showing how she experienced his behavior as well as how she constructed her own responses. Whitman's posture of control is evident early on, prior even to the couple's official engagement, as in the first line of a letter referencing their dating relationship: "How's it feel to be tied down to the same fellow for 4 months, 1 day, 23 hours, and 35 minutes? I sure am glad I tied down that little dropper of mine." His fixation on a precise moment of "capture" and a third-person reference to Kathy as a "little dropper" together undermine his inquiry about her feelings. A sentence shortly afterwards supports this interpretation, as he critiques her latest letter: "Miss Leissner I have a bone to pick with you [...] if I want to read typewritten paper I can find plenty of it at the ROTC building" (12 June 1962, *Select Letters*).

Proprietary demands pepper Whitman's communication, and his sweetness or politeness always betrays an agenda. He treats Kathy's social connections as his own from the beginning: "Oh, ask Floyd [the Justice of the Peace] if he can sell me liability insurance. I am having some trouble here. [...] Find out and let me know if he can insure me" (9 June 1962, *Select Letters*). His requests reinforce Kathy's expected menial or secretarial roles, such as sewing a patch on his karate outfit, taking care of floor mats for his new car, keeping track of clothing he left here or there, sending him a tinted photo of herself, cleaning their new apartment "the way she likes it," and wedding preparations—including a task traditionally performed by the groom: purchasing the wedding bands.

Whitman also casts himself as "expert" in odd ways, advising Kathy, for example, about getting a "premarital exam" because he'd seen an article in Modern Bride. (This after she has already informed him that she saw the family doctor.) He directs her to "get her teeth in good shape" because she won't be covered under his military dental policy, adding another comment that describes Kathy as a material property rather than a person: "Your dad's sure getting stung isn't he. Getting you ready to give to someone else" (24 July 1962, *Select Letters*).

By age twenty-one, Whitman was already heavily conforming to a paternalistic mode of relating to women, applying emotional pressure to get his way. His intention to marry simply emboldened and legitimized this "adult" posture. On occasions when Kathy's parents—particularly her father—raised doubts about a hasty wedding date, or whether Whitman should be allowed to stay overnight at their home, he pouts: "If I'm going to cause trouble I'd rather not come" (19 June 1962, *Select Letters*). The same letter includes an ultimatum to Kathy that pre-figures what he will write to his in-laws four years later: "I don't mean to hurt your Mom and Dad by taking you away, but if you marry me I'll expect you to go with me."

Letters written by Kathy and her mother reveal that there was a significant crisis within the first six months of marriage, due to what Kathy's mother called Whitman's "desire to dominate Kathy"—a desire revealed, in part, by his assertion that she "need[ed] to see a psychiatrist" because she had "changed" and was unhappy (qtd. in Scott-Coe "Listening"). Kathy's subsequent actions and letters indicate in various ways that while her husband continued to practice an ethos of control, she was testing her independence. Kathy initially left her family in February 1963 to withdraw from UT and join her husband on active duty in North Carolina, but after six months she also managed to get away from him and return to Texas, her family, and school when he was deployed to Cuba—despite disapproval from her in-laws as well as pressure from Whitman to have a baby (Scott-Coe "Listening").

Kathy's letters to Whitman during their separation (July 1963–Dec. 1964) provide many examples that demonstrate how she had internalized her husband's displeasure and adjusted to his preferences, even when it meant questioning her own judgment. In a long letter after their first anniversary, she apologizes for making him mad and for complaining about not hearing from him, pledging not to "nag" him about his gambling. She also downplays a more intimate, and sad, concern: "Please don't think I still have that dumb notion of your only desiring me for sexual release" (Letters 27 Aug. 1963). However, the longer Kathy lives apart from Whitman, the more deeply her writing expresses desires for change in their relationship (Scott-Coe "But What Would She Say?"). She explores one of his insecurities at length in a letter dated 6 May 1964:

[Y]ou think it's dependence but really that's the way it should have been when you first thought you were in-love with me [...]. [I]t's going to be almost like getting to know each other again when you get out [...]. [W]e are both going to have to realize that when we get back together and respect each other's new ideas. [n. pag.]

In another letter the following month, she worries that the "awful nice things" he said about her from a distance could be ominous:

> Honey, when your [sic] not with someone you love, it's awful easy to build them up to something they aren't and I'm afraid this may be what you're doing. I even got this impression when you were home on leave in May. You seemed a little dissatisfied with me in some ways and I really am the same girl you married. I may be unjustified in my fear but it could happen. (Letters, 13 June 1964)

Kathy's insight and her "fear"—framed cautiously around a specific recollection of his "dissatisfaction"—are poignantly attuned to the dangerous nature of the pedestal Whitman had placed her upon. In a different marriage, the couple's reunion in December 1964 might have brought Kathy's "new ideas" of "respect" and mutuality to fruition. Instead, Kathy's college diploma and professional status as a certificated science teacher would become threatening evidence to Whitman that she could thrive without him—and that she was capable of eluding his control.

The Problem of the Gender Pedestal

Whitman's use of a pedestal to elevate and to "measure" Kathy is documented in the diary he returned to after killing her. The entry dated 23 Feb. 1964, composed as he completed his sentence of hard labor following his special court martial, is often cited as proof of his affection. A more attentive reading, however, shows exactly how Whitman defined love, gender relations, and Kathy herself. The note he scrawled at the top—"I still mean it"—can only be interpreted favorably if we ignore the content of the entry he identified for posterity as important (Daily Record of CJ Whitman).

By framing our attention, Whitman sought to publicly perform his private ownership of Kathy; thus, his presentation enacts a pornographic aesthetic. Encompassing approximately four pages, the entry is one of the longest in a diary where the author left three-fourths of the pages blank. From the beginning, he writes of Kathy in terms that emphasize her use to him, twice repeating the phrase "most versatile" to describe her, and adding that she is "everything [he] want[s] in a wife," "the overall package," "the ultimate in a mistress," and "my most precious possession" (Daily Record). Furthermore, he includes cooking, sewing, and driving among her skills, as well the ability to learn quickly in sports or games.

Whitman's perspective is entirely reductive, with the first two pages itemizing Kathy's physical traits in comparison to "professional standards," for which—according to him—she comes up lacking: "not beautiful," "too short," not "a model's figure," "her knees and thighs are heavier than they should be" (Daily Record). He then selects certain parts as his to reshape ("we will be able to trim her legs down to the right proportions") and dismembers other body parts he approves of, which he isolates for competition "against any recognized bathing beauty." Ironically, he adds that his wife "is prone to feel inferior when she is in competition," as if his assessments had nothing to do with insecurities she felt about her body or her intelligence.

When it comes to their intimate life, Whitman refers to what he gets rather than gives, crediting himself for his wife's "sexual prowness [sic],"commenting that "her naivety [sic] in the first place is pretty responsible for her success at this venture [...]. I have taught her how to please me, which she does so expertly" (Daily Record). He talks of sex in a depersonalized way—as a "venture" at which one "succeeds"—with Kathy merely being the winning contestant for his desire. He does not recount shared experiences or mutual discoveries.

Equally significant is how the entry explicitly positions Whitman as the superior male authority when assessing Kathy's character compared to other women's: "When I stand back and judge her," he writes, "it amazes me that such a young woman can possess such outstanding qualities" (Daily Record). He highlights her "common sense," an "important asset which so many women do not have." Predictably, his definition is entirely self-serving: "she detaches herself from her emotions and desires in spite of what she would like to do [...] quite extraordinary for her sex." Here, gender stereotypes substitute for specific women, and he counts himself lucky compared to other men, who "have to put up with nagging temperamental wenches who will not use common sense [...] to realize that what their husbands are doing is correct." Yet Whitman composed this entry while suffering serious military consequences for "incorrect" choices of his own, including the gambling that had worried his wife six months earlier. He seems vaguely aware that while he may be entitled to judge, he also falls short of his own standards. He writes that he hopes "to be worthy of" Kathy, and that "maybe someday [he]'ll be able to convince [her] of all the emotions and feelings." He also casts the possibility of his own failure "by society's standards" as a failure against Kathleen.

A scattering of other journal entries describes their relationship in zero-sum, high-stakes terms that do not bode well: "live and die as man and wife," "she is my whole life," and "without her, life would not be worth living." While in the brig awaiting his court martial, he expresses a morbid, clinical view of death: "I have thought very much about the concept 'death.' When it overtakes me someday I must remember to observe it closely and see if it is as I thought it would be" (Memoranda 13 Nov. 1963). He also links Kathy, fatefully, to moral responsibility and self-control, describing how thoughts of her "kept him from beating the hell" out of a military policeman who interrupted him on the phone (Memoranda 22 Jan. 1964), and later writing that "she is really what keeps me straight" (Memoranda 30 Jan. 1964). Interestingly, Whitman appropriates Kathy's moral authority as his own, emboldening more harsh judgments against others and allowing him another arena for competition: "Everyone I meet seems to look at me in awe when they realize I don't run around [...]. [I]t ought to set some kind of record" (Daily Record of CJ Whitman 6 Mar.). When his boss questions him, Whitman reflects: "I couldn't convince him of how much Kathy means to me or how little sex with some whore means to me now that I have matured" (Daily Record of CJ Whitman 6 Mar.).

One long entry dated 13 March 1964 begins with how "Kathy would have been proud" of him for rebuffing sexual advances from another woman at Jazzland, a nightclub he frequented (and where he appeared to be employed in some capacity, likely as a bouncer): "I notice other women only to compare them with Kathy. They are all so far below her standards, she has them beat by miles" (Daily Record of CJ Whitman) At times, he transforms his standards to Kathy's, then projects his notions of "possession" onto her, writing: "Now that I am married, I feel as though I am her personal property and whenever another female touches me that she is violating my wife's property."

Letters from Kathy dated before and after this time (21 Feb., 23 Feb., and 28 May 1964) suggest that Whitman actively shared stories of past and present women while at the same time instructing Kathy "never to mention" them. He thus cast himself as a victim while also posing, sadistically, as judge for Kathy's reasonable insecurity.

By re-centering his final attention—and ours—on these paradoxes of possession and ever-elusive courtship, idealism and inadequacy, competition and failure, Whitman underscored how volatile these values could become. By identifying Kathy with the "angel in the house" from a long distance, he also made her vulnerable to gendered judgments, even gaslighting her, as "madwoman in the attic" upon their reunion. Worst of all, his pedestal made Kathy a primary target for elimination when his "common sense" ultimately dictated that violence was best.

[...]

Conclusion

Narrative erasure of domestic injury or killing in American stories of public violence perpetuates a social injustice: repeated silencing of private victims who are usually women. We must reconsider how "softened" or selective depictions only make women's deaths more palatable, especially at the hands of men who claim to love them. Mid-century sexism may appear quaint when we compare it to the misogyny expressed so freely in contemporary social media forums, but we have inherited its violent legacy. Fifty years after Whitman murdered his wife and mother before ascending the UT tower to shoot at strangers, American voters elected to our highest public office a man caught on tape bragging about grabbing women "by the pussy" (Mathis-Lilley). Attitudes that degraded, ranked, and separated women more than a generation ago continue to impact daily lived experience in ordinary domestic spaces—in bedrooms, offices, and on college campuses—whether or not anyone points or shoots a gun. Importantly, gendered entitlement transcends political identification, as demonstrated by the "volatile" and abusive background of James T. Hodgkinson, who in June 2017 shot at Republican congressmen practicing on a baseball field (Turkewitz, Stolberg, Eligon, and Blinder).

Domestic terror is a matter of women's lives and public health, and it is past time to notice the connection between what happens, how we talk about it, and what we are able to remember. Writing of an estimated sixty-six thousand women killed by men every year, Rebecca Solnit refers to femicide as an ultimate erasure: "Such deaths often come after years or decades of being silenced or erased in the home, in daily life, by threat and violence. Some get erased a little at a time, some all at once. Some reappear" (71). Kathy has been able to "reappear" because her brother, Nelson, protected the primary documents that preserved his sister's voice and perspective. When we do not question how and why domestic violence is subordinated to public spectacle, we unintentionally perpetuate the abuser or killer's perspective about when and how women's lives and deaths matter. We must re-attune our awareness so that gendered and sexualized violence no longer seems, by distorted comparison, a minor detail or narrative footnote, despite the reality of its massive and continued collective impact.

"Men often have to look outside of themselves for their first definition of what it means to be a man, so much so that it often leaves men in a dark and sad state of existence."

Cis-Men Must Embrace Their Authentic Truths

Jonathan P. Higgins

In the following viewpoint, Jonathan P. Higgins argues defining what it means to be a man is problematic for cis-men. They call for teaching men not to view masculinity as superior to femininity but as dangerous without it. They also believe men should not fear their masculinity in whatever form it comes and that they must embrace their own authentic truths. Dr. Jonathan P. Higgins is a speaker, writer, and social justice advocate. Their work has been featured on On Being, Slate, Huffington Post, OUT, SYFY, and others. They hold an Educational Doctorate in Leadership in Justice from the University of Redlands.

As you read, consider the following questions:

1. What other definitions of "man" does this viewpoint offer?
2. How can the phrase "man up" be harmful?
3. Should cis-men create their own definitions of "man?"

I can recall the first time that I asked the question, "What does it mean to be a man?" to a group of young men I was doing healing work with. In this particular situation, the young men were sharing their feelings about an exercise that each of them had just experienced, focused on the misogyny, sexism, and patriarchy that women often face in society.

Many of the young men shared that they immediately wanted to cry after the experience. Upon asking them why it seemed that they were emotionless during the exercise, they shared that they didn't allow themselves to exhibit such emotions because they needed to be strong for the other men in the group. The phrasing of "needing to man up" was used over 50 times, so much that I was not only exhausted, but perplexed.

It wasn't the first time I had heard the term "man-up" being used to describe the need that young men have to hide their emotions. I had been told to "man-up" by a family member after I said I didn't want to play football (or any sport really). I was also told that I needed to "man-up" after I found out my best friend died in the 9th grade and again after I experienced my first rejection letter to college.

I hear the phrase "man-up" used so frequently, I often wonder in what context the word "man" is being used and what it really says about how society views masculinity as a whole.

For years, I have grappled with this idea of maleness and masculinity from both a social and political lens. Society rarely provides space for men to be whole. Consider the "idea" of what it means to be a man in our society. When we define maleness, or masculinity, we are quick to assume that to be a man means being aggressive, loud, violent, and dominant. Even more, maleness and masculinity is often defined by one's gender, their gender presentation, and how they perform maleness and masculinity. Something that I have always found to be disturbing is how much of maleness and masculinity depends on one's genitals and what cis-gender men choose to do with said parts (and who they choose to do it with).

A common notion that is often not discussed when examining men and masculinity is how much emphasis is put on the performative aspect of being a man.

Very rarely are cis-men given space to interrogate and create their own definition of masculinity that includes being emotionally/mentally sound and whole. Men often have to look outside of themselves for their first definition of what it means to be a man, so much so that it often leaves men in a dark and sad state of existence.

From sports to the playground, masculinity is coded with phrases like "boys will be boys" or my personal favorite, "that's just how boys/men are." The emotionally damaging "masculinization" of young men starts even before young men have a keen sense of self; often before they even have the developmental capacity to fully understand the binary (gender vs. performance of gender.) These gender roles and expectations of gender performance are often given out like candy, without a child being able to fully comprehend what they're ingesting.

This notion that to be a man means being angry or emotionally unavailable has always been something that intrigued me. As both a queer and Black man, I often question where these ideas began and why people continue to hold them in such high regard. As I continue to battle with the true definition of what it means to be a "man" and how heteronormative (and homonegative) the definition continues to be, I recognize that the toxic notion of masculinity is forced on young cis-men before they even know how to properly tie their shoes.

I can remember hearing conversations between my mother and my uncles about how fearful they were for me because I didn't exhibit the behaviors of masculinity. I was emotionally available, somewhat shy, and enjoyed connecting with people on a deeper level. Somehow, that was seen as effeminate and the men in my family worked tirelessly to "make me harder," common rhetoric used in the Black cis-male community.

It behooves me to say that the root definition of what it means to be a man or to perform masculinity here in America

Abuse and Mental Illness

Abuse and mental illness can coincide. There are cases of individuals who have mental illness and are also abusive to their partners. There are also many individuals who have a mental illness and are healthy and supportive partners. If your partner does have a mental illness and is abusive towards you, it's important to keep in mind that the mental illness and abusive behaviors need to be addressed separately by the abusive partner. It is the abusive partner's responsibility to seek out support and create their own plan for managing their mental illness and be accountable for their abusive behavior. If your partner is not owning up to their actions, is not admitting to how much they're hurting you, and is not seeking out professional help then that's a sign that your partner isn't willing to change. If that's the case, then the abuse in the relationship tends to continue and escalate over time.

"Abuse and Mental Illness: Is There a Connection?" by Alexander, The National Domestic Violence Hotline, May 6, 2015.

continues to be grounded in oppression, marginalization, and white supremacy. As I have done my own work to unlearn the toxic nature of masculinity, I now comprehend that the harm being done to many young cisgender men, specifically young white cisgender men, is often connected to noxious ideals of power, positionality, and the want/need for cisgender men to be seen as a dominant gender. I am even more certain of this with the reports of gun violence transfixing us here in the U.S.

In challenging masculinity as a harmful and sometimes deadly social construction, we have to acknowledge that being viewed in society as masculine is reputed as a gift, while being viewed as feminine is a curse. Even with all of the negative ideologies of maleness and masculinity that cisgender men (and society) consume, being seen as a "man" means being free from critique and the need to unlearn elements of sexism and patriarchy, even in moments when you are the reason for someone else's struggle and pain.

Films like *The Mask You Live In* and *Tough Guise 2* examine the concept of performative masculinity and shine light on the lack of accountability that comes with maleness. They examine how young men are wired to "wage war" from a young age and encouraged to lean into concepts related to social dominance hierarchies. Cis-men, specifically cis-heterosexual men, are encouraged to take up any and all space, without questioning whether they are fully deserving of it.

A struggle that I have had as a queer cis-man of color is comprehending what maleness and masculinity means for me. I have never presented myself as a masculine. My voice is soft, I have always been called "pretty," and I am highly emotional — all things associated with femininity.

Though I have every right to be an aggressively violent person because of the things I have experienced as a queer Black man, I have chosen to unlearn maleness and masculinity as something ferocious. In my quest to redefine maleness and masculinity, I have started to understand that being a man means doing a great deal of self work.

My definition of "being a man" challenges me to speak openly and honestly about my thoughts and feelings. It's relearning how to speak from a truly genuine and unapologetic place. It's seeking out regular psychological therapy — something that many cis-men, specifically cis-Black men are taught not to do. But most important, it's knowing how to be honest with myself about where my pain and trauma begin and working through it to heal.

Before challenging others to learn what it means to "man-up," I would challenge everyone to unlearn what it means to be a man in our society and find a definition that allows cis-men to be happy, whole people. We must teach men not to see maleness and masculinity as superior to femininity, but dangerous without it. We must engage men to stop seeing their maleness and masculinity as being something that they should fear, while encouraging them to embrace their full authentic truth.

It is only then that we can truly create a healthier definition of what it truly means to be a man.

"It may well be the case that men are somewhat more biologically prone to violence and aggression, but we exaggerate this with a culture that shames men for even the slightest emotional display."

Lack of Emotional Expression Can Lead to Violent Behavior

Michael Carley

In the following viewpoint, Michael Carley argues that emotional expression is a necessary part of being a man. But this very trait is often shut down by parents and other adults. Instead, boys are instructed to "man up." Meanwhile, if a girl shows tomboy traits, she receives praise. A restricted set of emotional expressions only leads to problematic social isolation and depression, stress, suicide, and other conditions. Michael Carley is associate director, Institutional Research & Reporting, at Porterville College in Porterville, CA. He holds a master's degree in Sociology from Stanford University.

"Commentary: What Is Toxic Masculinity?" by Michael Carley, *Porterville Recorder*, March 21, 2018. Reprinted by permission.

As you read, consider the following questions:

1. Without expressing their emotions, how might men act out?
2. How do shame and bullying affect masculinity?
3. How might toxic masculinity affect college completion?

In a column nearly two years ago, I used the phrase "toxic views of masculinity" to describe one of the many causes of a mass shooting. At least one reader took exception to the phrase and I realized that I hadn't really defined it.

Academics and activists have begun using the term "toxic masculinity" quite commonly, but I haven't yet seen a good definition. So, I'll try to provide one myself.

First of all, let's say what it is not. No one is saying that all masculinity or that men themselves are toxic or bad. You are free to like the things that men stereotypically like: sports, cars, the opposite sex, with no judgment. There is nothing wrong with these things.

When does masculinity become toxic? When it derives from a rejection of the perceived opposite, femininity, that is so pervasive as to become unhealthy for both men and those around them.

Women and children are often victimized by toxic masculinity, through domestic violence and other violence, but men are victimized by it as well. Toxic masculinity stunts their cognitive, intellectual, and emotional growth. This damage is part of what fuels the victimization of women.

By rejecting anything stereotypically feminine, men and boys are taught to reject an essential part of themselves, something that is to be valued. What's more, these allegedly female traits are often ones that help us all get along in society, things like compassion, empathy, even politeness. A man or boy displaying these traits can invite ridicule.

Boys are taught from a very early age to reject all things feminine, from the color pink to television shows or movies that feature girls as primary characters.

Consider that when a girl "acts like a boy," she is often praised. Celebrity women proudly describe themselves as "tomboys" when they were young, a badge of honor.

What's the reverse equivalent of a tomboy? The word most commonly used is "sissy," though there are worse ones. Rather than a badge of honor, acting like a girl is a point of shame.

Boys are taught, often as toddlers, and often by both parents, not to cry. They must "man up" long before they can think of calling themselves men. Most displays of emotion, other than anger, are deemed suspect.

The result of this is men who do not know how to express themselves, who lack emotional intelligence. Many act out in ways, large and small, that are not healthy, either for themselves or for those around them. This may result in violence, but also takes the form of excessive risk-taking. More male babies than female are born each year (at least 105 boys to every 100 girls), but within a few years, risky behavior begins to take its toll, whether it be extreme sports, violence, or drag racing. There is a reason insurance companies charge young men very high rates.

Women far outlive men, but not primarily because they are healthier overall, but because they take fewer risks.

There is an area where women make healthier choices: even food has become gendered and men who choose salads risk ridicule for eating something insufficiently manly.

What's the biggest common denominator in mass shootings? Weapon type? Mental illness? Nope. Almost all of the perpetrators are men. Women suffer mental illness at roughly the same rate as men, but almost none commit large-scale violence.

It may well be the case that men are somewhat more biologically prone to violence and aggression, but we exaggerate this with a culture that shames men for even the slightest emotional display.

Toxic masculinity affects a variety of other areas of life as well, from education—men are falling far behind women in college completion—to the workplace, where men are discouraged from certain fields and limited in their growth in others due to inappropriate learned behaviors.

My friend Mark Greene, author of *Remaking Manhood*, has written extensively on this subject. He compiled a 30-second video that showed the downward cycle of emotional suppression imposed on men. It begins with shame and bullying, leading to a narrowing of the range of acceptable emotional expression. This results in a variety of problems, from increased stress, substance abuse and addiction, depression and suicide, and epidemic levels of several related diseases.

Adult men deal with very high levels of social isolation due to stunted development and a lack of meaningful friendship networks.

Luckily, there is pushback, led by people like Mark, and a variety of others from varying perspectives. As he wrote in another recent piece, it's not that masculinity itself is toxic, but "our narrow, conformist, violent, bullying version of it is."

It's time to change that.

"Men often face different reactions from society when disclosing rape and have different obstacles that prevent them from coming forward."

Male Rape Victims Do Not Speak Up

Johnny Loftus

In the following viewpoint, Johnny Loftus argues that while society still does not offer an adequate response to rape for either men or women, male rape victims in particular do not seek help for fear of negative perceptions. The author holds that such perceptions include not being considered men anymore. Shame is pervasive. To blame for this silence, he contends, are toxic gender norms. Johnny Loftus was a senior staff writer for the Campanile, *the Palo Alto, California, student-run newspaper.*

As you read, consider the following questions:

1. What factors contribute to the silence of male rape victims?
2. What risk of rape do men face in prison?
3. According to the study presented, when do the majority of male rape cases occur, during childhood or adulthood?

"Toxic Gender Norms Silence Male Rape Victims," by Johnny Loftus, the *Campanile*, December 6, 2017. Reprinted by permission.

Since the exposé of Harvey Weinstein, sexual assault has dominated news reports. Most recently came the suspension of James Levine of the Metropolitan Opera, who is accused of sexually assaulting two men when they were teenagers. The conversation, sparked by hashtags like #MeToo, has opened up spaces for women to talk about the sexual harassment and assault they have faced. However, with the exception of Levine's case, male victims of sexual assault have been largely absent from the conversation.

While it is true that, on average, women experience sexual assault and rape at much higher rates than men, the experience of sexual assault still affects men significantly. Men often face different reactions from society when disclosing rape and have different obstacles that prevent them from coming forward. The idea that men shouldn't be the ones being raped, male rape victims aren't "manly" enough or they should have been able to fight back are all common misconceptions that discourage male rape victims from coming out about rape. In reality, the event of men being raped is the same as it is for women. Being in a situation where you feel powerless and unsafe is traumatic for both men and women.

Society still lacks an adequate response to rape, for both male and female victims. Some women face comments saying they are sluts or that they "had it coming." According to a *New York Times* article, men who report rape risk appearing weak in the eyes of society, and because of this societal expectation that men should be strong, powerful and unemotional, male victims of assault may stay silent.

It's unfair that a man shouldn't be the one being raped, or that he should have been able to fight back.

Until 2012, national crime statistics on rape included only incidents against girls and women committed by men, according to a *New York Times* article. This idea that men are "strong" and "shouldn't be the ones being raped" remains prevalent in national organizations.

Male-on-male rape is littered with issues regarding sexuality. While homosexuality has become less of a taboo topic, straight men who are raped fear being labeled as "gay." Society has historically used the word "gay" as an insult, usually to suggest being homosexual makes one weak, overly emotional or otherwise feminine. The shame associated with this term stems from a long history of viewing feminine traits as inferior to masculine ones.

According to Neil Irvin, executive director of the organization Men Can Stop Rape, in a *New York Times* article titled "Men Struggle for Rape Awareness," "If you're sexually assaulted, there's this idea that you're no longer a man. The violence is ignored, and your sexual orientation and gender are confronted."

Sexual abuse in prisons is even worse. Inmates are at risk for assault from both prison guards and fellow prisoners. According to a report from the Bureau of Justice Statistics titled "Sexual Victimization in State and Federal Prisons Reported by Inmates, 2007," 4.5 percent of state and federal inmates reported sexual victimization in the last 12 months. With the national prison population of 1,570,861, the report suggests that 70,688 inmates experience sexual abuse annually.

Though there is more acknowledgement for the sexual abuse of male minors, children who experience abuse are reluctant to come forward because of the pressures put forth by society. In an interview with the *New York Times*, Dr. David Lisak, a clinical psychologist who has experience with interpersonal violence and sexual abuse, said there is "cultural blind spot about this [male sexual assault].

"We recognize that male children are being abused, but then when boys cross some kind of threshold somewhere in adolescence and become what we perceive to be men, we no longer want to think about it in this way."

Society sees children as more vulnerable. It is more willing to be sympathetic to male children who are raped when compared to adult males who are raped. However, even then, children fear coming out because of shame; many think the assault is their fault, or people will ostracize them.

According to a study in Virginia in 2009, 91 of 705 men surveyed experienced sexual assault, with the 94 percent of the assaults occurring when the men were minors. Of the men assaulted, fewer than one-fifth have ever received services related to their assault.

Both male and female victims of rape can experience shame, depression or even suicidal thoughts stemming from their assault. Victims are also at an increased risk for substance abuse, depression, interpersonal relationships and other health problems.

However, there is a lack of resources for male survivors, as many crisis centers do not even carry the resources to help men who are victims of assault. Of the few that do exist, the most prominent are the organization Male Survivor and the National Sexual Assault Telephone Hotline (1-800-656-4673).

Society needs to do a better job when it comes to individuals who come out with their experience of rape. We should not ignore women survivors, but we need to pay attention to all the male survivors as well.

"His claim to manhood was announced to every witness on and around the baseball diamond with the gasps and cries of that fallen runner."

Physical Aggression Gets Rewarded Among Eight-Year-Olds

Elan Justice Pavlinich

In the following viewpoint, Elan Justice Pavlinich uses the story of Toby, an eight-year-old dreamer on the softball field, to illustrate the process of masculinity construction in boys. Toby's coach tells him to "man up" when he misses a ball as shortstop. Fueled by his coach's admonition, he hits the next runner with a ball and feels elated by his accomplishment. Later at a fast-food restaurant, he opts for the toy fairy in the kid's meal, but the server thinks Toby has made a mistake and also gives him the red toy car. Elan Justice Pavlinich holds a doctorate in English literature from the University of South Florida.

"Man Up: Observing the Social Construction of Boys' Masculinity," by Elan Justice Pavlinich, *Graduate Journal of Social Science*. http://gjss.org/sites/default/files/issues/full/GJSS%20Vol%2012-3.pdf.

As you read, consider the following questions:

1. What is the masculine environment at the game?
2. How does Toby react to his coach's statement of "Man up?"
3. How was Toby's act of hitting another player with a ball rewarded?

Toby gave his Aunt a big hug before he rounded the bend of the cement dugout and joined his teammates of eight-year old boys. The paved and dusty floor was littered with pleather gloves, each decorated with athletic insignia or super heroes, strewn along with caps, all black and yellow, each one indistinguishable from the others, apart from the initials marking the tags on the inside to ensure that each cap corresponds to one particular player. The boys stirred in the shade, scuffling about, pushing, jabbing, laughing. They craned their heads upwards, squinting into the sun to see the faces of the coaches, all men with stubble shading their faces just below the imprints of crows feet around the eyes, and light wisps of silver sprouting from their temples. The men talked sternly about nothing in particular, breaking the monotony of their poker faces with periodic and abrupt sounds that registered as something seeming like amusement. Most of the boys kept their distance, but maintained their attention on the menfolk. They feigned interest in their conversations about work, the renovations on Main Street, and the recent political scandal, but actually none of them understood the significance of any of this. Not the boys, nor the men who uttered these trivialities. The only strand of fascination that the young ones gleaned from this meaningless exchange of words was that this was guy talk. This is the stuff about which men converse. Performing comprehension equates to a kind of currency, and so if one acquires the currency, deploys the proper cues, one might be able to buy one's way into manhood. To talk with the big boys is to be one of the big boys. Toby kept to the corner in the shade, where he would not be assaulted by roughhousing, or lose his cap.

From this huddle, one of the coaches turned his head in the direction of the boys. Facing them, but not looking at them, he formed a small shriveled opening with his mouth and spit a streaming arch of filth that hit the cement of the dugout with a splat, congealed in an instant, and made of itself a point of convergence for the gaze of every lad looking for cues to compose their own identities in the image of the father. The pool of spit soon grew as each uniformed youth attempted to demonstrate the precision of his own expulsion of spittle. Some stood directly over the bubbled gob, as clear streams ran down their chins and dribbled with patters that sounded like footsteps creeping closer to their mark. It was something more than a demonstration of personal corporeal control, or the ability to aim and move matter in accordance with one's will. For some, it seemed, that by combining his own bodily fluid with that of the father's was like concocting an elixir. If his spit mixed with his spit, then they were one and the same. Toby watched nervously, and swallowed the lump in his throat.

Later, well enough into the game's innings that the spectators had forgotten how many were left, parents exchanged small talk, compared teachers, and took regular breaks to shout the name of their particular child whenever he took to home plate for an opportunity to crack the ball. Toby played shortstop when it was his turn in the field. He enjoyed this position because after the thrill of the game wore off in the first three innings, he was able to turn his attention to the soft dirt between first and second base. It was smooth, running through his fingers, and he thought to himself that if the granules were only a bit smaller this dirt would be more like liquid, a burnt-orange pool on which they could barely stand. He liked these moments of peace in which he could be alone in spite of the clamor and structured play around him, where he could feel the breeze and enjoy the simplicity of the clear sky and the soft dirt. Just then, an abrupt wind broke his self-indulgent solitude, and he realized that it was the game ball that had soared by his head. The shouting of teammates and parents pressed in on him. From the opposite direction another body moved quickly

Male Aggression Is a Serious Problem

Last week when I spoke to the students in my classroom about the mass killing at Marjory Stoneman Douglas High School in Florida, I started to cry. I didn't want them to feel hopeless. Yet, as I stood in front of a mix of 16-year-old boys and girls in my American Literature class and tried to support them in the face of another slaughtering of innocent people, I couldn't help but cry.

According to the U.S. Department of Justice, men commit the vast majority of violent crimes in this country. Every mass shooter we have seen in recent years has been a man. Some politicians are trying to divert our attention by blaming mental illness. Yet, if mental illness were the cause of this violence, then why do women rarely commit such horrendous acts? They suffer from mental illnesses, but they are not killing our school children. Males are. If congressmen truly want to see the root of the violence in American, they can start by looking in the mirror.

Part of the problem stems from how we teach masculinity. American culture celebrates aggression as a defining characteristic of what it means to be a man. We encourage male dominance. These messages are ubiquitous. We see them in sports, entertainment, the workplace, and politics. Our political leaders unabashedly disregard or outright excuse male violence against women. The violence we see in our country is a malignant outgrowth of our rigid definition of what it means to be a man.

If we honestly care to stop such male-initiated violence, men need to own up to their own aggression and find new ways of expressing masculinity. And we need our federal government to create strong gun laws that limit the ownership and sale of guns.

"It's Not Just About Guns. Male Aggression Is a Serious Problem," by Patrick O'Connor, *Editorial Projects in Education*, February 22, 2018.

by him. It was a runner. Toby missed the ball aimed at him, and the runner gained second base. "Get your head in the game!" his mother shouted from behind a chain-link fence on the sidelines.

"Man up," the coach said from the central location of the pitcher's mound, like an authority bearing down on him, both of them playing their part in some playground panopticon. Toby felt ashamed and afraid, like he had failed. The social order saw his flaws. He was a dreamer, and there was no time or exceptions made for a young man who could not engage the other fellows in their assigned tasks. Between first base and second base, he wanted that soft dirt to become liquid and permit him to sink and hide.

Toby averted his eyes from the father on the mound and strained to suppress his tears. Avoiding the feeling of emptiness opening in place of his guts, he focused all of his attention on the next play. The coach slowly pitched the ball at the next batter who swung awkwardly, relying on chance to connect his bat with the baseball. It did. With a sharp peel, the ball arched upward into the air, culling the attention of all those young men in uniform to squint past the oversized brim of their baseball caps, and calculate the trajectory of the plummeting mass. It came down in the outfield just before the batter made contact with first base. Toby intently watched his teammates scuttling to retrieve the ball as one boy in left field picked it up, looked deliberately in his direction, aimed and threw. The ball hit Toby's glove with a satisfying thud as the runner jogged past him towards second base. Coerced by the command to "man up," Toby put all of his strength behind his throw. He centered on his target with feigned but hopeful precision and hit his mark perfectly. The ball held Toby's shame and regret, but the dull thump that it made on impact resounded in his mind and echoed over the feelings of dread that he had only recently experienced. The runner went down into the dirt, instead of Toby, just after the ball took his breath from him by striking just between his shoulder blades. Toby was overjoyed. The runner was overcome. He was lifted by Toby's coach—just like a baby, Toby thought. The coach delivered the downed runner, gasping for breath and stained by tears mixed with fine burnt-orange dirt, to his mother on the other side of the chain-link fence.

The rest of the game passed quickly as Toby soaked in the exhilaration of accomplishment. He felt like he had earned his rank as a team member, as one of the other boys, but special. His mark was not composed of a pool of collective spit that would evaporate from the cement. His mark was made on the skin of the opposing team. He was accepted by them, as one of the boys. His claim to manhood was announced to every witness on and around the baseball diamond with the gasps and cries of that fallen runner.

Toby's peers congratulated him after the game. The coaches had very little to say beyond announcing the next time and place for their next practice session. With an orange slice in one hand and a juice box in the other, Toby trundled over to his Mom, and Aunt, and Grandmother. He asked if they could go out for a special treat, to celebrate his achievement like the coaches who met up at the tavern across the street for beers after the boys' game.

His Aunt took him to a local fast food chain where he got an ice cream cone for wearing his uniform in the restaurant and all of the meals from the kids' menu came with a little toy. This week the toys were either miniature automobiles or pocket dolls with freely moving strands of hair and fluorescent wings. Toby told his aunt that he wanted the fairy. They looked so pretty and fun. In his mind, the idea of pushing a piece of plastic across the floor while supplying revving sounds seemed so boring. Where was the toy car to go? How much fun is it to pretend to be seeking out a destination? And, should the toy ever arrive, would it not then be rendered obsolete. No, the fairy was more appropriate for him. Fairies represented possibility. Their wings were transportation, and once they arrived they had the means by which to facilitate imaginary dialogue, action—an entire narrative potential was embodied by the fairies.

Toby's Aunt let him order his own food. He enjoyed this responsibility. He even got to hold the money so that he could pay for everything. He felt smart and special as he informed the clerk that he wanted a kids' meal with a fairy. The young man behind the counter looked puzzled, like he hadn't quite heard the request. Toby felt self-conscious again, like maybe he wasn't ready to order his own food, like he was unintelligible or deficient. The clerk's eyes moved toward Toby's Aunt for comprehension. She nodded her head in affirmation and the young man processed their order. Toby not only paid for their meal, he also received the change, and counted it back to his Aunt as they waited for their food to be placed on the counter before them.

They sat together at the table and Toby parceled out their food while his Aunt asked him what he thought about today's game. She seemed concerned, but he was not. He was proud, and he was excited to unwrap his new toy before he started eating. With his Aunt, the rule was always that the toy was to be placed on the table, and only after he had made his best effort to eat everything would they then go outside and play with whatever the latest plastic loot happened to be that promotional season. So Toby pulled out the bag and was excited to see the bulbous shadowy eyes of a human face looking at him through the plastic. He was anxious to stretch that bag to point of tearing so that he could free the glittering wings that were hastily crammed into the packaging. With the toy set aside he removed the other contents of the box, including a burger, some fries, and something else. Something wrapped in plastic at the bottom of the box.

It was another toy. Toby was thrilled! In an instant his mind leapt to the possibility of fairy friends. Now that he had two, they would each have someone with whom they could speak. They could fly around the room, singing songs to which only Toby knew the lyrics. At night they would sleep together just above Toby's pillow on the headboard of his bed, so that he could look up at them before following their glittering wings into dreams.

He inspected the newfound treasure to see if his friends would be identical twin fairies, or if they would be entirely dissimilar. He had already hoped that this one would have the bright pink dress to go with the bright green dress of the other one whom he had already placed on the table. Instead, he saw shiny red. It was a car. The clerk called over to them from the other side of the counter. He explained that he wanted Toby to have both toys because he assumed that when Toby got home he would feel bad because he had picked the wrong toy. Toby didn't understand. The plastic car in the plastic bag didn't seem to amount to much. It did not signify anything the way that the fairy had. Toby felt bad when he looked at it. He felt bad about himself. Toby had not realized that he was wrong, but now he felt it.

Periodical and Internet Sources Bibliography

The following articles have been selected to supplement the diverse views presented in this chapter.

Bob Cook, "How Youth Sports Coaches, Parents Can Make Masculinity Less Toxic," *Forbes*, November 29, 2017, https://www.forbes.com/sites/bobcook/2017/11/29/how-youth-sports-coaches-parents-can-make-masculinity-less-toxic/#4443f125e690.

Lizz Darcy, "Toxic Masculinity in Sports," Unbalanced, July 2018, https://unbalanced.media/toxic-masculinity-in-sports.

Alia E. Dastagir, "Men Pay a Steep Price When It Comes to Masculinity," *USA Today*, April 26, 2018, https://www.usatoday.com/story/news/2017/03/31/masculinity-traditional-toxic-trump-mens-rights/99830694/.

Mark Greene, "How the Kavanaugh Hearings Model the Patterns of Assault," The Good Men Project, October 12, 2018, https://goodmenproject.com/featured-content/the-kavanaugh-hearings-mirror-assault/.

Mark Greene, "Why Manning Up Is the Worst Thing to Do," *YES Magazine*, December 3, 2015, https://www.yesmagazine.org/issues/good-health/why-manning-up-is-the-worst-thing-to-do-20151203.

Jenny Hong, "Gen Z Athletes Are Rejecting Hypermasculinity," Very Good Light, August 22, 2018, https://www.verygoodlight.com/2018/08/22/gen-z-athletes-are-rejecting-hypermasculinity-in-sports/.

Jessica Luther, "Football Won't Turn Boys into Men," Huffington Post, August 21, 2018, https://www.huffingtonpost.com/entry/opinion-football-toxic-masculinity_us_5b7c1237e4b0a5b1febf19c9.

Ryan Martin, "5 Things We've Learned about Men, Anger, and Aggression," *Psychology Today*, March 20, 2017, https://www.psychologytoday.com/us/blog/all-the-rage/201703/5-things-weve-learned-about-men-anger-and-aggression.

James W. Messerschmidt and Achim Rohde, "Osama Bin Laden and His Jihadist Global Hegemonic Masculinity," *Gender & Society*, 2018.

Chapter 4

Does Toxic Masculinity Affect Only Men?

Chapter Preface

Toxic masculinity is a learned set of behaviors, according to some experts. While boys learn to be physically aggressive, girls learn to be submissive. Toxic masculinity, then, may harm not just the men who exhibit these traits, but the women and children around them.

Studies show that men do not live as long as women. Some perspectives consider the biological and psychological aspects of the data in various countries around the world to try to come to some consensus. Some insist on biological and physical differences, such as a man's build, while some contend the differences come not from science but from socially constructed gender norms. With specific respect to acts of violence, although there may be no distinct biological difference between the sexes when it comes to a violence predisposition, there are other contributing factors that could include childhood trauma and group violence. The harm done to self and others may be due to a learned reluctance to speak up and ask for help when needed. A serious medical issue may be ignored because a man has learned to be stoic.

Such learned behaviors come at a price, even during youth. It may take years of concerted effort to appreciate one's own differences and to muster the courage to stay clear of others' toxic behaviors. Viewpoints illustrate how bullying may force some boys to develop hypermasculinity, which may mask their authentic selves and cause only more anger and aggression.

In the following chapter, viewpoint authors approaching the topic from a variety of professional and personal perspectives examine the various ways in which toxic masculinity may hurt men themselves, boys, girls, and women.

Viewpoint 1

> *"All of these anatomical, hormonal, behavioral and evolutionary factors demonstrate the biological, instinctual inclination of men to be more combative."*

Men Are Built for Aggression

Dorian Furtuna

In the following viewpoint, Dorian Furtuna argues that men are biologically geared toward aggression. Using evidence from theorists and research studies, he also points to how men and women are educated, emphasizing the social construction of gender roles. The author concludes that both biological and sociological factors contribute to the male predisposition toward fighting and violence. Dorian Furtuna, PhD, is an ethologist from the Republic of Moldova. He is interested in revealing the biological and instinctive foundations of human social behavior.

As you read, consider the following questions:

1. What evidence shown here supports the theory that men are more aggressive than women?
2. Has social emancipation of women led to more aggressive behaviors among them?
3. What roles does genetics play in determining aggression?

"Male Aggression," by Dorian Furtuna PhD, *Psychology Today*, September. 22, 2014. Reprinted by permission.

In almost every society men are the ones who are overwhelmingly involved in wars, in all kinds of intergroup aggressions and intragroup homicide; they mobilize themselves in armies of violent fans, in criminal gangs, in bands of thugs, etc. These observations are as old as the world and have allowed us to create a clear distinction between male and female sexes regarding their predisposition to violence. Wars are a biosocial product of men and a field for male's manifestation [Goldstein, 2001]. The same thing is true of crime and cruelty, which are closely linked to masculinity.

Canadian evolutionary psychologists Martin Daly and Margo Wilson, who specialize in studying the homicide phenomenon, have analyzed 35 homicide data sets from 14 countries, including some from primitive societies and some from different eras. Among these societies men committed homocide, on average, 26 times more frequently than women [Daly, Wilson, 1994]. Also, familicides (the killing of family members) are committed mostly by men. Some data have shown that men were involved in more than 90 percent of cases [Wilson, Daly, 1997, p. 160].

Men are also, in 70 percent of cases, the victims of homicides. In some societies, this percentage jumps to over 90 percent [Daly, Wilson, 1988; Berkowitz, 1993, p. 274, apud Buss, Duntley, 2002].

In the Russian Federation, in 1996, 86.6 percent of all serious crimes were committed by men. In the U.S., in 2004, 85 percent of total serious crimes were committed by men. Ninety-two percent of serial killers from the U.S. are men.[1] This statistical report is valid for most countries, regardless of their geographical location or size. In the Republic of Moldova, for example, about 90 percent of crimes are committed by men.[2]

Let us analyze another dimension of violence—cruelty and animal abuse. One of the studies that approached this issue found the following male-to-female ratio, regarding violence to animals: beatings—38 to 1, shooting—16 to 1, torture—20 to 1, burning—17 to 1 [Gerbasi, 2004].

Why are men more aggressive than women? Several theories have been proposed, trying to explain this phenomenon, most of

Society and Gender Roles

At a young age, you are taught to adhere to gender roles. Apparently, the sex you were given at birth determines many factors in your life. These factors include how you dress, behave, and express yourself. What if you do not feel comfortable with these gender roles, what if you do not 'fit in'?

Society in general will paint gender roles across your life with the illusion of what is 'normal' for your gender. No matter how you act, you will always be 'normal' for you. Every person is a unique being with a unique form of expression, and they should not be forced to stay in a box of what they should or should not do according to their sex. Gender does not have to be a binary, and gender does not even have to matter for every person. Your physical sex also does not determine your gender identity with finality. Humans are complex and should not be simplified. Break out of these gender roles, speak out against stereotypes, and find your own person among the masses.

"Toxicity of Gender Roles," by Chris, mindyourmind, February 9, 2015

them being from social psychological theories. One of the most popular theories belongs to American social psychologist Leonard Berkowitz. According to him, men and women are educated, traditionally, to carry out different social roles. Berkowitz uses the following reasoning for his theory: Think of all the ways in which modern Western society teaches children that fighting is more suitable for men than to women. Folk literature and the media constantly present men, and not women, fighting. Parents buy toy guns for boys and dolls for girls. Parents are more willing to endorse and encourage the aggressive behavior of boys, and not of girls. Again and again, directly and indirectly, minors learn that men are aggressive, and women not [Berkowitz, 1993, p. 395].

The theory of "social roles" has created a new paradigm in gender policies and marks, even today, the ways in which many civic and preschool education strategies are developed. It is presumed that girls and boys shall be educated and treated alike, non-discriminatory, and even the behavioral differences between them will disappear. However, although it contains in itself a good dose of truth (boys and girls were, traditionally, part of a different education), Berkowitz's theory about learned social roles was subject to several critics, who have shown its vulnerabilities.

First of all, it's not the parents that impose behavioral styles on their children, but their reaction at the latter's requests; toy guns are bought for boys and dolls for girls because these are usually the children's preferences (in part genetically predetermined). And as parents respond to children's preformed wishes, so do media, offering a content which corresponds to behavioral patterns already existing on a social level [Hoyenga, Hoyenga, 1993]. Then, Berkowitz's theory mirrored the Western culture, but didn't take into account the realities from other cultures (without cinema, literature, media, toy stores), where the behavioral patterns of boys still greatly differ from that of girls. It was noted, among other things, that homicides in North America (where it seems that the media fosters intense social roles) are marked by sex differences to a lesser degree than in many other societies [Daly, Wilson, 1989, p. 101–102, apud Buss, Duntley, 2002]. So it is not the imprinting of social roles that sits at the origin of men's increased aggressiveness, but inner causes, determined by the nature of men.

Also important in this regard are the findings of social psychologists who have noted that the social emancipation of women in recent decades has barely influenced or enhanced the expressiveness of aggressive behavior in women, which is additional proof that the higher degree of masculine aggressiveness is, first of all, due to genetic factors. Sex differences predetermine, on a genetic level, the differences in aggressive behavior [Wilson, Herrnstein, 1985]. It's specific for women to use verbal aggression in intrasexual competition between women and rarely are there cases of physical assault. Women use only language in competitive strategies [Buss, Dedden, 1990, apud Fitzgerald, Whitaker, 2009, p. 469].

Most relevant in explaining the genesis of male aggressive behavior proved to be the approaches from an evolutionary perspective. Thus, the fact that men are more aggressive and stronger than women can be explained through intrasexual competition (between males). Men have inherited these skills from our evolutionary ancestors, because, in general, in the living world, gaining a higher hierarchical status, resources, protecting the family and obtaining competitive advantages in conquering women involves increased physical contest and increased aggressiveness [Buss, Duntley, 2006; Gat, 2010]. Similarly, in many animal species, including primates, males have the biological role of being guardians of the territory and of banishing the intruders or of protecting the group from predators, and these functions imply that males exhibit a higher level of aggression than females [Wilson, 1975].

The fact that males are more aggressive and more violent is reflected by their anatomy itself; in many animals species they are heavier, more muscular, better armed with means of attack and defense. In humans, for example, the arms of men are, on average, 75 percent more muscular than those of women; and the top of a male body is 90 percent stronger that the top of a female body [Bohannon, 1997; Abe et al., 2003, apud Goetz, 2010, p. 16]. Also, men are taller, they have denser and heavier bones, their jaw is more massive, their reaction time is shorter, their visual acuity is better, their muscle/fat ratio is greater, their heart is bulkier, their percentage of hemoglobin is higher, their skin is thicker, their lungs bigger, their resistance to dehydration is higher, etc. In other words, from all points of view, men are more suited for battle than women, and these skills are native; they were selected and evolutionary polished [Sell et al., 2012, p. 33].

Men also have a specific hormonal status. Testosterone, for example, is directly responsible for inducing competitive and even criminal behavior. According to Evolutionary Neuroandrogetic Theory, male sex hormones (androgens) are correlated with the increased ability of males to acquire resources, hierarchical position and sexual partners [Ellis, 2003, 2004].

All of these anatomical, hormonal, behavioral and evolutionary factors demonstrate the biological, instinctual inclination of men to be more combative. Therefore, on an individual and social level, men are involved in acts of violence and crime. The social environment only cultivates and points out these predispositions towards fighting and aggression.

Sources

1. http://murders.ru/Florida_2.html

2. Statistica gender // Biroul Național de Statistică al Republicii Moldova / http://www.statistica.md/category.php?l=ro&idc=264

Abe T., Kearns C.F., Fukunaga, T. Sex differences in whole body skeletal muscle mass measured by magnetic resonance imaging and its distribution in young Japanese adults // British Journal of Sports Medicine. Vol. 37. 2003. P. 436-440.

Berkowitz L. Aggression: Its causes, consequences, and control. New York. McGraw-Hill. 1993. 485 p.

Bohannon R.W. Reference values for extremity muscle strength obtained by hand-held dynamometry from adults aged 20 to 79 years // Archives of Physical Medicine and Rehabilitation. Vol. 78. 1997. P. 26-32.

Buss D.M., Dedden L.A. Derogation of competitors // Journal of Social and Personal Relationships. Vol. 7. 1990. P. 395-422.

Buss D.M., Duntley J.D. Murder by Design: The Evolution of Homicide // Behavioral and Brain Sciences. 2002 / http://www.philosophy.dept.shef.ac.uk/AHRB-Project/Papers/Non-pdf-papers...

Buss D.M., Duntley J.D. The Evolution of Aggression // In M. Schaller, J.A. Simpson, D.T. Kenrick (Eds.), "Evolution and Social Psychology." New York, NY: Psychology Press. 2006. P. 263-285.

Daly M., Wilson M. Homicide and cultural evolution // Ethology and Sociobiology. Vol. 10. 1989. P. 99-110.

Daly M., Wilson M.I. Evolutionary psychology of male violence // In: Male Violence (Ed. by J. Archer). London: Routledge. 1994. P. 253–288.

Daly M., Wilson M.I. Homicide. Hawthorn: Aldine de Gruyter. 1988.

Ellis L. Genes, criminality, and the evolutionaryneuroandrogenic theory // In: A. Walsh and L. Ellis (Eds.), "Biosocialcriminology: Challenging environmentalism's supremacy Hauppauge." NY: Nova Science. 2003. P. 13-34.

Ellis L. Sex, status, and criminality: A theoretical nexus // Social Biology. Vol. 51. 2004. P. 144-160.

Fitzgerald C.J., Whitaker M.B. Sex differences in violent versus non-violent life-threatening altruism // Evolutionary Psychology. Vol. 7(3). 2009. P. 467-476.

Gat A. Why War? Motivations for Fighting in the Human State of Nature // in P. Kappeler and J. Silk (eds), "Mind the Gap: Tracing the Origins of Human Universals". Springer Berlin. 2010. P. 197-220.

Gerbasi K. Gender and nonhuman animal cruelty convictions: Data from Pet-Abuse.com // Society and Animals. Vol. 12. 2004. P.359-365.

Goetz A.T. The evolutionary psychology of violence // Psicothema. Vol. 22(1). 2010 Feb. P. 15-21.

Goldstein J. War and gender: How Gender Shapes the War System and Vice Versa. Cambridge: Cambridge University Press. 2001.

Hoyenga K.B., Hoyenga K.T. Gender-related differences: Origins and outcomes. Boston: Allyn & Bacon. 1993.

Sell A., Hone L.S., Pound N. The importance of physical strength to human males // Human Nature. Vol. 23(1). 2012 Mar. P. 30-44. doi: 10.1007/s12110-012-9131-2.

Wilson E.O. "Sociobiology: A New Synthesis." Harvard University Press. 1975.

Wilson J.Q., Herrnstein R.J. Crime and Human Nature. New York. Simon & Shuster. 1985.

Wilson M.I., Daly M. Familicide: uxoricide plus filicide? // In M Riedel & J Boulahanis, eds., Lethal violence: Proceedings of the 1995 meeting of the Homicide Research Working Group. Washington DC: National Institute of Justice. 1997. P. 159-169.

Viewpoint 2

> *"To ensure that our fathers, brothers, sons and friends stop dying prematurely, we need to fundamentally rethink what being a 'man' is all about."*

Toxic Masculinity Leads to Earlier Deaths Among Males

Haider Javed Warraich and Robert Califf

In the following viewpoint, Haider Javed Warraich and Robert Califf argue that men die earlier than women for psychological, biological, and psychobiological reasons. In terms of physical health, they contend, a man's man may be the worst thing a person could be. Haider Javed Warraich is a cardiovascular disease fellow at Duke University Medical Center in North Carolina. He is also the author of Modern Death: How Medicine Changed the End of Life. *Robert Califf is a professor and vice chancellor at Duke University. The former commissioner of the Food and Drug Administration, he also holds a leadership position at Verily Life Sciences.*

As you read, consider the following questions:

1. What factors lead to men dying earlier than women?
2. How are characteristics of toxic masculinity harmful to aging men?
3. According to this viewpoint, how do Asian men stand out culturally?

For much of recent history, men have tended to die earlier than women, though this was not always the case: for many centuries, the perils of childbirth effectively nullified any advantage women had over men. But modern medical care has dramatically reduced maternal death, and women in most countries now have a consistent advantage in life expectancy compared with men.

According to the most recent US data, the average American man dies five years before the average American women, and even wider gaps are seen among different racial and ethnic minorities: for example, Asian American women live 16.5 years longer than African American men on average.

While disparities in life expectancy between men and women have typically been greeted with a collective shrug, these questions are taking on greater urgency as new research reveals ominous trends for men's health. Researchers from Stanford demonstrate that in societies where maternal mortality from childbirth has improved and birth control reduces family size, women consistently outlive men.

In addition, the gap in life expectancy continues to widen with increasing income inequality. Although the gap in life expectancy had started to narrow in the 1970s, the overall death rate is again climbing, particularly for white American men, making it essential to understand why the state of men's health is going from bad to worse.

Many people assume that shorter male lifespans are driven, directly or indirectly, by genetics and other biological factors. Yet a closer look at science, medicine, and culture suggests that the engine for this disparity might be the long-held ideal of masculinity itself. It is becoming increasingly clear that a "man's man" might be the most dangerous thing a man can be.

Fundamental biology may indeed play a role in disparities in life expectancy, and many theories have explored this possibility. The higher rate of male births has been suggested as one reason for differences in survival, as has the need for better female health to ensure successful child-rearing.

The additional X chromosome carried by women might provide "backup" in the event of some genetic abnormalities. Higher levels of estrogen in women protect the heart from disease, and higher heart rates in women could simulate the beneficial effects of exercise.

On the other hand, increased risk-taking is associated with higher levels of testosterone in men. Males, too, show greater susceptibility for infections. These are just some of the hypotheses that have been advanced to explain differences in lifespan.

However, wide variation in life expectancy suggests that it is the behaviors and attitudes associated with gender, rather than the biological differences associated with sex, which are responsible for men dying sooner than women. For instance, the gender gap in lifespan favors women by 11.6 years in Russia, but approaches zero not only in some poor countries such as Mali but also in some high-income regions such as Santa Clara, California.

Furthermore, a study published earlier this year found no significant difference in the proportion of elderly trans men and non-trans men in the US, implying that behaviors stereotypically associated with male gender might explain why men are more likely to die younger than women.

Male behaviors and attitudes that affect their health—including notions about when it's OK to seek help—are not fixed byproducts of genes and hormones, but are strongly influenced by culture. A traditional masculine ideal common in the US holds that "the most powerful men among men are those for whom health and safety are irrelevant."

How Masculinity Is Killing Men

All of the oldest living people in the world are women. On average, men die five years sooner than women, and they also are more likely to die from cancer. While some have theorized that men are just biologically doomed, researchers at Rutgers University think that toxic masculinity is to blame.

In a new study titled, "Masculinity in the doctor's office: Masculinity, gendered doctor preference and doctor–patient communication," published in *Preventative Medicine*, Mary Himmelstein and Diana Sanchez set out to find out why men have shorter life expectancies and are more likely to suffer from several leading causes of death. Expanding on scientific literature that links toughness and avoidance of weakness with negative implications for health, among other traits associated with male norms, Himmelstein and Sanchez found that men who adhere to the traditional scripts of masculinity and hold the belief that manhood is precarious—or that it could be "lost"—were more likely to choose a male doctor over a female doctor due to implicit bias. In turn, men who consulted with a male doctor were less likely to have open and honest conversations about their medical health, which is an integral step in early detection and preventative care. In other words, men who "tough out" minor health problems because they believe that going to the doctor is a sign of weakness are, in part, killing themselves.

"How Masculinity Is Killing Men," by Gabby Bess, Vice Media LLC, March 25, 2016.

These ideals, a fatal concoction of risky behavior, anti-intellectualism, and unwillingness to seek help are reinforced by portrayals of masculinity in popular culture that emphasize "toughness, self-reliance, and stoicism" while tending to erase images of male aging and infirmity.

This traditional view of male identity comes with serious health consequences. Men are more likely to smoke and drink than women and therefore are more likely to suffer from health problems related to these behaviors. Importantly, not only are men less likely to see a doctor, they are also much less likely to seek psychological help. This is one of the main reasons why suicide rates, both intentional and unintentional from drug overdoses, remain much higher for men than women, and continue to rise.

While men are much less likely to attempt suicide, they are unfortunately much more likely to succeed when they do so, because of their preference for firearms. These issues are only becoming more urgent as the economic dislocations created by the transition to a knowledge-based economy continue to place additional stresses on US culture and communities.

It seems paradoxical that a segment of the US population that has historically enjoyed greater power and privilege can also be considered vulnerable. But unexamined assumptions about biological determinism, compounded by cultural ideas about masculinity, have created a situation that places men at risk for worse health outcomes from a surprisingly early age.

The internalization of a male identity in which seeking help is seen as a sign of weakness begins in childhood and becomes particularly intense during adolescence.

This maladaptation is reflected in widening gender gaps in educational achievement, with girls outperforming boys not only in the United States, but around the world. These gaps persist throughout the educational experience, leading to concerns that boys are not being prepared for success in the modern economy.

At the same time, however, studies show that what men consider "manly" varies by culture, and therefore might be modifiable. When researchers interviewed white patients who had survived a heart attack, they concluded that their "fears of being seen to be weak contributed to delays in seeking medical care and led to reluctance to disclose symptoms to others."

Yet the same study found that South Asian men "emphasized wisdom, education and responsibility for the family and their own health as more valued masculine attributes, and this contributed to a greater willingness to seek medical help".

To help close the gap in lifespans between the sexes, a public health campaign with support from the private sector is needed to help reshape what it means for men to seek medical and psychological help.

This might take the form of educational interventions, starting at an early age, that offer an idea of maleness in which seeking help from others is seen as a positive attribute, as well as increased mindfulness of the potential harmfulness of language and images that valorize self-destructive "masculine" behavior.

All of these considerations should occur within a research enterprise that addresses the gender survival chasm as a multifactorial issue that includes biological, psychological and psychobiological issues.

To ensure that our fathers, brothers, sons and friends stop dying prematurely, we need to fundamentally rethink what being a "man" is all about.

Viewpoint 3

> *"When we acknowledge how systemic, ingrained toxic masculinity comes into play, what do we do? When we see that even our loved ones can be complicit in upholding male dominance, what do we do?"*

Toxic Masculinity Is Systemic and Ingrained

Mattie Wyndham

In the following viewpoint, Mattie Wyndham argues that a cultural system produces toxic masculinity. Based on her own episode of sexual coercion and subsequent work as a researcher on the Colby Healthy Masculinities Project, she has come to understand that men are raised to show aggression and have little emotion. Men who want to resist unhealthy behaviors may find it difficult to do so. Mattie Wyndham has served as a research assistant in the Colby College Resistant Masculinities Project since 2015. She is a graduate of Maine's Colby College with a bachelor's degree in Women's, Gender, and Sexuality Studies

"How Can #MeToo Address Toxic Masculinity?" by Mattie Wyndham, Women's Media Center, January 23, 2018. Reprinted by permission.

As you read, consider the following questions:

1. According to this viewpoint, what are some of the toxic masculinity behaviors?
2. How did this author discover that the problem is systemic?
3. Should we accept the failure of men to overcome toxicity?

"Have you heard?"

My roommate asks me this just as I walk through my creaking dorm room door, before I even have the chance to heave my backpack off. It could have been any day in October or any day since.

Have I heard about James Franco?

No, but has she heard about Aziz Ansari?

We rehash tired, but still fairly genuine, lines of disappointment, as we are so used to doing in this post-Weinstein era. We rehash, but often without renewed anger; such stories of sexual misconduct are not new to us; we know the sexual assault epidemic personally. The stories of sexual harassment and assault I've heard from nearly every woman I know on campus vary in terms of exact details but provoke all too similar emotions. Some of my best friendships here at Colby College were born from nights filled with the domino effect of post-assault panic attacks and subsequent caretaking.

My own assault during the fall of my first year of college left me angry. Being forced to sit through two classes with my perpetrator the following spring shook my very values. You see, my perpetrator is an activist. He takes every anthropology class offered about revolutions and human rights. He attends events on sexual violence prevention. It was not a violent rape; I called it a "bad hook-up" for months before I realized what happened was sexually coercive. When it happened, I felt like all of my friends were hooking up, but I had never even taken off my bra in front of a man before. He knew that. I did not know how to speak up and say no louder and sharper and, really, I did not know how to separate my desires from my expectations. It was cultural coercion, too.

At the time, I did not know how to understand his coercive behavior and believe my experience and my own trauma. I worried humanizing him would delegitimize my own experience and found myself paralyzed by the daily dilemma of choosing which of our experiences to validate. Where I once held steadfast to the theory that radical love and forgiveness were better than punishment and rage, in the dining halls, in my Title IX meetings, and especially in those classes with him my first-year spring, I would often recall that he had three other Title IX complaints against him and feel angry.

During my sophomore year, however, I had lengthy discussions with femme friends that opened my eyes to where my perpetrator's coercive behavior had come from—despite his supposed dedication to activism. My friends and I began to talk more about how even the so-called "good" men on campus—men who publicly condemned toxic masculinity—would still speak over women in sexual violence prevention meetings, constantly mansplain everything from rape culture to the wage gap, and, in some cases, romantically pursue women long after they told them to stop. I realized that some of my closest male friends—men who proclaimed to have a healthy understanding of masculinity—were actually emotionally manipulative, and in fact used their self-proclaimed titles of "good" men as evidence for why their habits of manspreading or slyly belittling Hillary Clinton couldn't possibly be sexist. I began to see the real ways the intent of these men did not align with the impact of their actions, but didn't know what to do about it.

For the past two and a half years, I have been working with Professor Mark Tappan and fellow student researchers on the Colby Healthy Masculinities Project. This work involves identifying men who embody healthy masculinity and trying to understand how they developed that mindset. This work has helped me see the way my perpetrator is a product of a system that encourages toxic masculinity—or the way that men are raised to be stoic and aggressive, and to ensure their dominance over women at any cost.

I now understand that even for men like my perpetrator—men who want to and even try to resist unhealthy masculinity—it's often difficult to do so. This reality is perhaps most evident when it comes to sex; sex between men and women is particularly complicated and messy because the different levels of power men and women have in our society is complicated and messy.

Just as my initial coping mechanism post-assault was to demonize my perpetrator and eschew nuance in the name of healing, I worry that perhaps that has been our wider cultural approach. It's great that we have begun to hold perpetrators accountable, but the way in which we have done so adheres to a logic that men exist in an uncomplicated binary: those who are good and those who are bad, and only bad men rape. If we can get rid of Weinstein, Moore, Lauer, Spacey, Franco, then, we reason, we'll be safe. But when we finally understand that it is more than just a few bad apples committing these atrocious crimes, when we acknowledge how systemic, ingrained toxic masculinity comes into play, what do we do? When we see that even our loved ones can be complicit in upholding male dominance, what do we do?

We should be speaking up, and the current reckoning we're witnessing and participating in should be happening. Anger and a reordering of power structures are necessary, good parts of this battle. But we must also process the nuances of misogyny and toxic masculinity. I believe we have to acknowledge that all men are affected by and act out male dominance in a variety of ways every day. Instead of criminalizing individual "bad" men, maybe we can make space to accept that men were raised in a culture that systemically normalizes sexual coercion and devalues women's voices. Being raised in this culture means that many men will act along these lines not because they are evil, but because this is what they have been taught to do. They will fail us.

But perhaps we can accept this failure. Maybe we can acknowledge that the process of unlearning male dominance cannot reasonably be one free of failure. The cultural need to see gender performed "correctly" encourages the masculine hierarchy, but dismissing notions of perfection and seeing failure as an opportunity for growth may encourage a cultural shift toward systematic change.

To be clear, we cannot excuse men when they fail. Accepting that men will fail does not mean allowing them to forgo accountability. In fact, it asks them to be accountable for their failure rather than defensive about it.

We must process that our friends, family, and heroes may be complicit in a system that hurts us. We must accept all of this and push men to be better if we ever want them to succeed.

Viewpoint 4

> *"There is no conclusive evidence that men and women differ in their innate biological or psychological propensity for violence."*

Social Environment Dictates Why Men Commit Majority of Violent Acts

Ian Hughes

In the following viewpoint, Ian Hughes argues that the social environment causes men to commit most of the violent acts, although both men and women are equally capable of violence. He examines a possible set of contributing factors that may cause more male violence. These factors include childhood trauma and group violence. However, he concludes that gender construction is to blame. Ian Hughes, PhD, is author of Disordered Minds: How Dangerous Personalities Are Destroying Democracy *(2018). He is a Research Fellow at the Environmental Research Institute, University College Cork. He lives in Dublin, Ireland.*

As you read, consider the following questions:

1. Are men and women both victims of violent crime?
2. How do groups influence individual behavior?
3. Is toxic masculinity an abnormality?

"Why Are Men More Likely to Be Violent Than Women?" by Ian Hughes, Journal Media Ltd, February 26, 2015. Reprinted by permission.

Whether it is in acts of personal violence such as rape or murder, or group violence such as rioting, gangland murders or war, men play a role that far exceeds that of women. But why is this?

Consider the facts.

Men are the major perpetrators of violent crime. Data from the United States for the period 1980 to 2008, for example, shows that men were responsible for 90% of the murders committed during that period.

Men are also the major victims of violent crime. The same US data shows that 77% of the murder victims over those same two decades were men.

Women, on the other hand, are more likely to be the victims, rather the perpetrators, of violent crime.

The Figures Are Staggering

In fact, the degree to which women are the victims of male violence is truly staggering. Women aged 15 to 44 worldwide are more likely to be killed or maimed because of male violence than because of war, cancer, malaria, and traffic accidents combined.

In the US alone, the number of women murdered as a result of domestic violence between 9/11 and 2012 exceeded the number of terrorist victims on that day and all American soldiers subsequently killed in the War on Terror combined.

Male violence against women is one of the invisible and under-recognised pandemics of our time.

What is it that makes men more likely to be violent than women?

What Causes Violent Behaviour?

In seeking explanations, it is important to recognise that violence cannot be explained in terms of a single cause. Instead there are multiple possible factors that contribute to violent behaviour.

One possible factor is biology. Research shows that persistent violent offending is often correlated with minor brain damage or certain psychological abnormalities, particularly psychopathy.

A second possible contributing factor is childhood trauma. There is strong evidence that severe neglect and violent abuse in childhood are high risk factors for violent behaviour in adults. It is abundantly clear that grossly dysfunctional parenting can cause acute problems in child development, which in turn can result in delinquent behaviour, including violence.

The Significance of Group Violence

A third possible contributory factor is the influence of groups on individual behaviour.

Research into group violence, such as racial and homophobic assaults, has shown that violent groups are typically made up of four different types of offenders: thugs for whom violence is their normal means of resolving disputes; xenophobes who blame others for their own troubles; sympathisers who become involved through peer pressure; and politically motivated offenders, who are usually educated and indulge in violence in pursuit of their political beliefs.

In organised gang violence, financial rewards from lucrative illegal activities such as drug dealing, human trafficking, and prostitution provide an additional powerful incentive for gang membership. Poverty, high unemployment and lax law enforcement provide the context within which violent gangs can thrive.

A further possible explanation for violent behaviour is given by sociological theories of violence. One such argument is that capitalism encourages egoism and greed, rather than altruism, and provides a supportive culture for violence. Moreover, the argument holds, in capitalist societies the rich are in a position to engage in large-scale fraud, or to launch full-scale wars for personal gain, secure in the knowledge that they will escape punishment.

Gender Construction

Whatever the range of factors contributing to violent behaviour—brain damage, psychopathy, childhood trauma, the influence of groups, or societal context—it is clear that they affect men to a larger degree than women.

This brings us a final possible contributing factor, and one which can have markedly different effects on men and women—gender construction.

Research on gender strongly suggests that many of the differences between men and women that we take for granted are something we are taught rather than something we are born with.

According to Lise Eliot of Chicago Medical School, for example, infant brains are so malleable that small differences at birth become amplified over time through parental and societal reinforcement of gender stereotypes. Girls, Eliot holds, are not naturally more empathic than boys. They just get to practice these feelings more.

By age five, most boys and girls will have internalised the gender roles and expectations taught them by their families, schools, religions and societies. And in many instances, boys will have been socialised for violence by being taught that being a man means being tough, powerful, intimidating, and a stud.

While constructions of masculinity differ widely both within and between countries, it seems clear that some constructions of masculinity increase the chances of boys growing up to become violent men.

Neither Gender Is Innately Predisposed to Violence—Social Environment Is Key

The evidence so far available suggests two important conclusions.

First, there is no conclusive evidence that men and women differ in their innate biological or psychological propensity for violence. The fact that men commit the majority of violent acts may instead be understood as arising mainly from the social environment.

Second, the fact that explanations of persistent violent behaviour are to be found to varying degrees in brain damage, psychological abnormality, childhood trauma, group peer pressure, and adverse social environments allows us to go one step further and conclude that persistent violent behaviour is an abnormality that emerges under certain circumstances.

Under the patriarchal circumstances that currently prevail worldwide, this abnormality emerges in men to a much greater degree than in women.

Empowerment

So what to do? A lot, of course, is already being done. In keeping with the fact that violence has multiple causes, those working on solutions are doing so on multiple fronts.

Four types of peacemaker stand out.

The first are the many groups worldwide working to empower women. Violence against women is most likely when the power differential between men and women is large. Enforcing women's rights to equality in domestic, economic and political relationships is therefore key to reducing violence.

However, since there is no conclusive evidence that women are inherently less violent than men, empowering women without changing the widespread acceptance of violence in society can only be part of the solution.

Hence three other types of peacemaker are crucial.

First, the forces of law enforcement, whose role is to remove persistent violent offenders from circulating in society and to provide a credible deterrent against violent behaviour.

Second, those working to redefine masculinity so that boys grow up believing that being a man can also mean being gentle, nurturing and empathic.

And third, those opposing violence in all its forms by pressing for non-violent solutions to human conflicts. This group realises that violence traumatises and embitters and its use continually creates ever more violent individuals.

Together these peacemakers are working towards a world in which violence is seen as an abnormality—an abnormality from which both men and women can be equally immune.

Viewpoint 5

> *"Incels seek to prove themselves to other men, or to the unrealistic standards created by men, then blame women for a problem of men's own making. Women become threats, cast as callous temptresses for withholding sex from, in their perception, deserving men."*

The Incel Rebellion Is a Retreat to Classic Male Domination

Ross Haenfler

In the following viewpoint Ross Haenfler argues that the burgeoning incel movement is nothing more than a response of frustration felt by some men who fall short of society's idea of masculinity. The author maintains that this supposed rebellion is nothing new, that frustrated misogynists have been committing acts of violence against women since the beginning of time. Yet he emphasizes its inherent danger: The viewpoint was prompted by recent acts of violence committed by men supposedly aggrieved by rejections by women. Ross Haenfler is Associate Professor of Sociology at Grinnell College.

"How a Masculine Culture that Favors Sexual Conquests Gave Us Today's 'Incels,'" by Ross Haenfler, The Conversation, June 6, 2018. https://theconversation.com/how-a-masculine-culture-that-favors-sexual-conquests-gave-us-todays-incels-97221.

As you read, consider the following questions:

1. What is an "incel"?
2. What do the sociologists mentioned in the viewpoint mean by "aggrieved entitlement"?
3. Why does the author caution against dismissing incels?

After the recent shooting at the Santa Fe, Texas, high school, the mother of one of the victims claimed that the perpetrator had specifically killed her daughter because she refused his repeated advances, embarrassing him in front of his classmates. A month prior, a young man, accused of driving a van into a crowded sidewalk that killed ten people in Toronto, posted a message on Facebook minutes before the attack, that celebrated another misogynist killer and said: "The Incel Rebellion has already begun!"

These and other mass killings suggest an ongoing pattern of heterosexual, mostly white men perpetrating extreme violence, in part, as retaliation against women.

To some people it might appear that these are only a collection of disturbed, fringe individuals. However, as a scholar who studies masculinity and deviant subcultures, I see incels as part of a larger misogynist culture.

Masculinity and Sexual Conquest

Incels, short for "involuntary celibates," are a small, predominately online community of heterosexual men who have not had sexual or romantic relationships with women for a long time. Incels join larger existing groups of men with anti-feminist or misogynist tendencies such as Men Going Their Own Way, who reject women and some conservative men's rights activists, as well as male supremacists.

Such groups gather in the "manosphere," the network of blogs, subreddits and other online forums, in which such men bluntly express their anger against feminists while claiming they are the real victims.

Incels blame women for their sexual troubles, vilifying them as shallow and ruthless, while simultaneously expressing jealousy and contempt for high-status, sexually successful men. They share their frustrations in Reddit forums, revealing extremely misogynist views and in some cases advocating violence against women. Their grievances reflect the shame of their sexual "failures," as, for them, sexual success remains central to real manhood.

The popular 2005 film "The 40-Year-Old Virgin" nicely illustrates the importance of sexual success, or even conquest, to achieving manhood, as a group of friends attempts to rectify the protagonist's failure while simultaneously mocking him and bragging about their own exploits. "Getting laid" is a rite of passage and failure indicates a failed masculinity.

Cloaked in the anonymity of online forums, incels' frustrations become misplaced anger at women. Ironically, while they chafe under what they perceive as women's judgment and rejection, they actually compare themselves to other men, anticipating men's judgment. In other words, incels seek to prove themselves to other men, or to the unrealistic standards created by men, then blame women for a problem of men's own making. Women become threats, cast as callous temptresses for withholding sex from, in their perception, deserving men.

Entitlement

If heterosexual sex is a cultural standard signifying real manhood for a subset of men, then women must be sexually available. When unable to achieve societal expectations, some lash out in misogynist or violent ways. Sociologists Rachel Kalish and Michael Kimmel call this "aggrieved entitlement," a "dramatic loss" of what some men believe to be their privilege, that results in a backlash.

Noting that a disproportionate number of mass shooters are white, heterosexual and middle class, sociologist Eric Madfis demonstrates how entitlement fused with downward mobility and disappointing life events provoke a "hypermasculine," response of increased aggression and in some case violent retribution.

According to scholar of masculinity Michael Schwalbe, masculinity and maleness are, fundamentally, about domination and maintaining power.

Given this, incels represent a broader misogynist backlash to women's, people of color's and LGBTQI people's increasing visibility and representation in formerly all-male spheres such as business, politics, sports and the military.

Despite the incremental, if limited, gains won by women's and LGBTQI movements, misogyny and violence against women remain entrenched across social life. Of course not all men accept this; some actively fight against sexism and violence against women. Yet killings such as those in Toronto and Santa Fe, and the misogynist cultural background behind them, remind many women that their value ultimately lies not in their intelligence and ideas, but in their bodies and sexual availability.

Fringe Men or Mainstream Misogyny?

Dismissing incels and other misogynist groups as disturbed, fringe individuals obscures the larger hateful cultural context that continues in the wake of women's, immigrants', LGBTQI's and people of color's demands for full personhood.

While most incels will not perpetrate a mass shooting, the toxic collision of aggrieved entitlement and the easy availability of guns suggests that without significant changes in masculinity, the tragedies will continue.

The incel "rebellion" is hardly rebellious. It signals a retreat to classic forms of male domination.

"The fact is, almost no trait, masculine or otherwise, is inherently good or bad. Yes, some of the traits warned about in the APA's report can have positive manifestations. … However, each of these traits also has a dark side."

Let's Have a Dialogue About Masculinity

Aaron Pomerantz

In the following viewpoint Aaron Pomerantz argues that media reaction to the American Psychological Association (APA) 2018 report on boys and men has shown a misunderstanding of the APA's conclusions. The author maintains that the media's interpretation of the report has inflamed the hot button issue of toxic masculinity and, instead of encouraging the reasonable discussion that could be had, has further alienated the public on the issue of masculinity. Aaron Pomerantz is a social psychologist and doctoral candidate at the University of Oklahoma, where he studies culture, the legal system, and the psychology of religion.

"What the APA's Report on Men and Masculinity Really Tells Us: A Psychologist's Perspective," by Aaron Pomerantz, Foundation for Economic Education, January 12, 2019. https://fee.org/articles/what-the-apas-report-on-men-and-masculinity-really-tells-us-a-psychologists-perspective/

As you read consider the following questions:

1. What is wrong about the reaction to the APA report on Boys and Men according to the author?
2. What do the norms of a "real man" depend on according to the viewpoint?
3. How can some traits be seen as both positive and negative?

Because we didn't have enough to be angry about, this week brought us another subject for outrage: the American Psychological Association (APA) hates men. The APA's Guidelines for Psychological Practice with Boys and Men (https://www.apa.org/about/policy/boys-men-practice-guidelines.pdf), published in August 2018, has come to prominence in the media, supposedly demonstrating psychology to be the latest social science to join the ranks of the war on men.

Upon deeper examination, however, this report should have served as a wonderful opportunity for dialogue regarding masculinity. The report reflects concerns raised by both sides of the political spectrum, and there is far more common ground than might be expected. However, rather than finding any opportunity for civilized discussion, the news media would rather engage in the typical strategies of oversimplification, exaggeration, and polarization that so define modern politics.

What the APA Actually Said

The APA report highlights a number of facts that many, such as Dr. Christina Hoff Summers, have raised previously. For example, men are more likely to commit and be the victims of homicide and are three times more likely to commit suicide. The report further outlines 10 guidelines for psychologists to consider in addressing these and similar issues.

Many of these guidelines should be uncontroversial regardless of your political orientation. Indeed, many of them have been talking points of the political right for several years, such as recognizing the importance of caring fathers in the family unit. Similarly, the report recognizes—and indeed emphasizes—that there is no single conceptualization of masculinity.

The norms of "a real man" depend on factors like age, ethnicity, and culture, each of which may provide its own specific challenges. The report focuses on psychologists learning to recognize and address these challenges in the treatment of men, as well as dealing with the antisocial phenomena that may result, such as unfettered aggression, misogyny, or emotionally restrictive norms like "boys don't cry."

Rather than calmly reporting the facts (heaven forbid!) or recognizing the common ground this report represents, both sides of the aisle seem hell-bent on making this into yet another divisive political issue. On the left, the response has been triumphant crowing about toxic masculinity and the dangers men pose to a civilized society. On the right, the response has been a reactive moral panic about how the left hates traditional manhood. Both of these responses are polarizing, oversimplified, and worst of all, useless.

Reactance on the Right

One particularly worrying response from the right is the assertion that the masculine traits "maligned" in this report, such as aggression, dominance, and the desire to be breadwinners, are positive and even desirable traits in "real" men. This response is called reactance, and it seems to define modern political discourse.

The fact is, almost no trait, masculine or otherwise, is inherently good or bad. Yes, some of the traits warned about in the APA's report can have positive manifestations, which the APA report already admits. Aggression can be positive when used to defend the self, the home, or the family unit. Dominance, in the proper dosage, can be an important part of leadership. The desire to provide can be an important part of maintaining a healthy family unit. However, each of these traits also has a dark side.

I sincerely hope it is uncontroversial to say that aggression is maladaptive, harmful, and immoral when it takes the form of spousal or child abuse. Dominance is likewise undesirable when it causes a predilection to start bar fights over minor insults. Even the desire to be the "breadwinner" can also be maladaptive if a man is uncomfortable when his wife makes more than him and it harms their relationship.

Again, I hope none of these facts would be considered controversial. However, it seems that in their reactance-fueled ire, many on the right would rather blindly assert these traits to be positive, never stopping to consider the potential negative consequences raised by the APA's report. With demonstrated potential risks like abuse, homicide, and suicide in play, such a reactive response seems foolish and dangerous.

Masculine Honor Ideology and the Dangers of Unchecked Masculinity

Much of my own research focuses on a specific set of cultural norms known as honor ideology, which highlights the dangers of unchecked, badly focused masculinity. In an honor culture, a man's worth is entirely measured by his willingness to engage in violent retaliation to insults or threats. Honor ideology has been consistently linked to many of the same phenomena raised by the APA's report, including needless risk-taking, stigmatizing mental health treatment, violence against women, and increased risk of suicide. In each of these cases, the norms and requirements of being a "real man" have real, concretely deleterious effects for men who subscribe to them or live in a culture where they are enforced.

Honor ideology is a widespread phenomenon in America, despite what some on the right claim about the harmful effects of masculinity being "outliers." Millions of men subscribe to these norms and suffer the negative effects of doing so, including the "gender role strain" mentioned in the APA's report. Failing to subscribe to honor norms makes one less of a man, which can lead to everything from mental health crises such as suicide to taking dangerous risks in order to regain "lost" masculine honor.

While not all masculinity is tied up in honor ideology, the phenomenon still serves as a concrete example of how masculinity and its associated norms can have severe risks for its adherents. These risks are not simply for "outliers."

Common Concerns and Common Ground

Obviously, not everything in the APA's report will be agreed upon by everyone of every political orientation. However, the report still contains a number of opportunities for finding common ground. The problems raised by the report are real, and they are not partisan. They afflict men across cultures, ethnicities, ages, and political persuasions. They are widespread problems, and they need a solution.

The goal of the report was to draw attention to the ways that masculinity can go wrong rather than to condemn masculinity outright.

The APA's Division 51 has even issued a clarification (http://division51.net/homepage-slider/twitter-message-not-reflecting-the-guidelines-for-boys-and-men/), highlighting the positive elements of masculinity and stressing the fact that the goal of the report was to draw attention to the ways that masculinity can go wrong rather than to condemn masculinity outright. However, it seems both sides of the political spectrum would rather ignore these common issues in favor of continuing the anger and polarization that define modern politics.

If you have not read the APA's original report, I encourage you to do so with fresh eyes. You may be surprised to find that your ideas, on either side of the political spectrum, will be challenged. Regardless, the problems raised by the APA report are not going away, and without finding common ground, it is likely that they will not be solved.

Periodical and Internet Sources Bibliography

The following articles have been selected to supplement the diverse views presented in this chapter.

Noah Berlatsky, "This Father's Day, Men Are Experiencing a Crisis of Masculinity. The Solution? More Feminism," NBC News, June 17, 2018, https://www.nbcnews.com/think/opinion/father-s-day-men-are-experiencing-crisis-masculinity-solution-more-ncna884051.

Hannah Cranston, "Toxic Masculinity is the REAL Cause of Mass Shootings, HuffPost, November 7, 2017, https://www.huffingtonpost.com/entry/toxic-masculinity-is-the-real-cause-of-mass-shootings_us_5a02786ce4b0230facb84147.

E.J.R. David, "Fathers, Let's Talk to Our Sons About Toxic Masculinity," *Psychology Today*, June 15, 2016, https://www.psychologytoday.com/us/blog/unseen-and-unheard/201606/dear-fathers-lets-talk-our-sons-about-toxic-masculinity.

Ayeke Fakie, "Toxic Masculinity Emboldens Women as Oppressors Too," Huffington Post, April 28, 2018, https://www.huffingtonpost.co.za/ayesha-fakie/toxic-masculinity-emboldens-women-as-oppressors-too_a_23421028/.

Donna Ferguson, "Authors Steer Boys from Toxic Masculinity with Gentler Heroes," The *Guardian*, July 14, 2018, https://www.theguardian.com/books/2018/jul/14/how-boys-can-grow-into-real-men-male-authors-fight-toxic-masculinity.

Michael Flood, "Australian Study Reveals the Dangers of 'Toxic Masculinity' to Men and Those around Them," The Conversation, October 15, 2018, http://theconversation.com/australian-study-reveals-the-dangers-of-toxic-masculinity-to-men-and-those-around-them-104694.

Jane Gilmore, "How Toxic Femininity Is Damaging Us," *Sydney* (Australia) *Morning Herald*, May 17, 2018, https://www.smh.com.au/lifestyle/life-and-relationships/how-toxic-femininity-is-damaging-us-20180517-p4zfvt.html.

Laura Kiesel, "Don't Blame Mental Illness for Mass Shootings; Blame Men," Politico, January 17, 2018, https://www.politico.com/magazine/story/2018/01/17/gun-violence-masculinity-216321.

Tyler Lehner, "Hypermasculinity Is Toxic: My Story of Being Bullied for Being Different," October 14, 2018, https://thoughtcatalog.com/tyler-lehner/2016/08/hypermasculinity-is-toxic-my-story-of-being-bullied-for-being-different/.

Donah Mbabazi, "The Effects of Toxic Masculinity," The *New Times* (Rwanda), October 4, 2018, https://www.newtimes.co.rw/lifestyle/effects-toxic-masculinity.

Jason Om, "Toxic Masculinity: Helping Men Understand the Impact of Their Behaviour," ABC Life, November 26, 2018, https://www.abc.net.au/life/toxic-masculinity-men-understanding-their-behaviour/9998310.

Annie Reneau, "Toxic Masculinity Hurts Us All. Here's How We Can Fix It," Scary Mommy, n.d., https://www.scarymommy.com/toxic-masculinity-raising-boys/.

Scott Simon, "Boys and Masculinity in America," NPR, September 29, 2018, https://www.npr.org/2018/09/29/652872401/boys-and-masculinity-in-america.

For Further Discussion

Chapter 1

1. Tracy E. Gilchrist discusses the kneejerk reaction that some—particularly men—have to the term "toxic masculinity." Why do you think some people can't see that "toxic" is used as a modifier and therefore is distinguishing a type of masculinity? Is there a better way to express the concept?
2. In her article, terra loire coins the term "tender masculinity," lists its characteristics, and presents book and movie examples. Are her arguments convincing? Why or why not?

Chapter 2

1. Josephine Jobbins maintains that men's need for physical strength and stoicism changed during Queen Victoria's reign. Do you agree that toxic masculinity dates back to this time—or earlier?
2. Fatma Özdemir Uluç bases her viewpoint on her work with students and teachers inside Turkish schools. How might her methods work in American schools?

Chapter 3

1. Johnny Loftus maintains that all too often rape victims remain silent. What prevents women victims from talking? What prevents men victims from talking? Ae these reasons the same or different and why?
2. Elan Justice Pavlinich tells the story of eight-year-old Toby on the softball field. How does this narrative illuminate toxic masculinity vs. an approach citing studies and statistics?

Chapter 4

1. Haider Javed Warraich and Robert Carliff point out that women live longer than men. How does the evidence they present make a convincing argument?
2. Mattie Wyndham joined a research team to more fully understand toxic masculinity after a sexual coercion incident. How might engagement in research activities help to understand what happened to her?

Organizations to Contact

The editors have compiled the following list of organizations concerned with the issues debated in this book. The descriptions are derived from materials provided by the organizations. All have publications or information available for interested readers. The list was compiled on the date of publication of the present volume; the information provided here may change. Be aware that many organizations take several weeks or longer to respond to inquiries, so allow as much time as possible.

American College Personnel Association—College Students Educators International

One Dupont Circle, NW
Suite 300
Washington, DC 20036
Phone: 202-835-2272
Email: info@acpa.nche.edu
Website: www.myacpa.org/scmm

The American College Personnel Association (ACPA) hosts the Coalition on Men and Masculinities. For more than 30 years, this coalition has served as a space to discuss the role of men's development as it relates to student affairs educators. Its goals include to promote awareness among men, women, and transgender individuals and to support men on campus to develop their full potential.

American Men's Studies Association

1080 S. University Avenue
Ann Arbor, MI 48109-1106
Phone: 470-333-AMSA
Email: amsamail@gmail.com
Website: mensstudies.org

The American Men's Studies Association is a group of scholars and researchers dedicating to the advancement of critical studies of men and masculinities. Although its roots go back to the 1980s, it officially formed in 1991.

American Psychological Association

750 First St., NE
Washington, DC 20002-4242
Phone: 800-374-2721
website: www.apa.org

The American Psychological Association represents psychology in America with more than 100,000 researchers, educators, clinicians, consultants, and students among its membership. It is the leading scientific and professional psychological organization in the United States. It publishes many articles in its journals, magazines, and website regarding harm reduction.

American Sociological Association

1430 K Street, NW
Suite 600
Washington, DC 20005
Phone: 202-383-9005
Email: asa@asanet.org
Website: www.asanet.org

The American Sociological Association was founded in 1901 and has more than 13,000 members worldwide. It has more than 50 special interest sections, including a section on race, gender, and class.

Center for the Study of Men and Masculinities

Stony Brook University
S404 Social and Behavioral Sciences
Stony Brook, NY 11794-4356
Phone: 631-632-7739
Email: centerformandm@stonybrook.edu
Website: www.stonybrook.edu/commcms/csmm/

The Center for the Study of Men and Masculinities, formed in 2013, engages in interdisciplinary research about boys, men, masculinities, and gender. Its goal is to bring researchers and practitioners together to develop an environment that fosters healthy masculinities and greater gender equality.

The Good Men Project

Email: info@goodmenproject.com
Website: goodmenproject.com

The Good Men Project was founded by Tom Matlack in 2009. It comprises a diverse community of thought leaders engaged in conversation about men's changing roles and how those changes affect others. The project tackles these roles from a variety of perspectives that reinforce the multiple dimensions of masculinity.

The ManKind Project

Phone: 800-870-4611
Email: outreach@mkp.org
Website: mankindproject.org

The ManKind Project is a nonprofit organization with 30 years of success in developing and implementing positive life-changing programs for men. The organization provides training and education as well as a network of more than 900 free support groups. It operates in 22 countries.

Men's Resource Center for Change

236 North Pleasant St.
Amherst, MA 01002
Phone: 413-253-9887
Email: mrc@mrcforchange.org
Website: www.mensresourcecenter.org

The Men's Resource Center incorporated in 1988 and offers programs, projects, and services to support a new vision of masculinity. Its website features a number of informational editorials. The organization provides classes and training to high schools, universities, and others throughout the Northeast. In 2003 it began an annual four-day walk to stop domestic violence.

MeToo Movement

Email: info@metoomvmt.org
Website: metoomvmt.org

MeToo Movement was founded in 2006 to help victims of sexual violence. This grassroots organization has grown since the #metoo hashtag brought sexual harassment to the national stage. The organization connects survivors to resources.

National Organization for Men Against Sexism

3500 E. 17th Avenue
Denver, CO 80206
Phone: 303-997-9581
Email: info@nomas.org
Website: nomas.org

The National Organization for Men Against Sexism is an activist group of both men and women who support positive changes for men. The organization hosts the Healthy Masculinity Action Project and also hosts an annual conference. It encourages challenges against male stereotypes and advocates for a more robust set of characteristics.

Bibliography of Books

Clementine Ford. *Boys Will Be Boys: An Exploration of Power, Patriarchy, and the Toxic Bonds of Mateship*. Crow's Nest, New South Wales, Australia: Allen & Unwin, 2018.

Stewart Hoover. *Does God Make the Man? Media, Religion, and the Crisis of Masculinity*. New York, NY: New York University Press, 2015.

Lewis Howes. *The Mask of Masculinity: How Men Can Embrace Vulnerability, Create Strong Relationships, and Live Their Fullest Lives*. Emmaus, PA: Rodale Wellness, 2017.

Ronald F. Levant and Joel Y. Wong. *The Psychology of Men and Masculinities*. Washington, DC: American Psychological Association, 2017.

Edward Morris and Freeden Oeur (eds.). *Unmasking Masculinities: Men and Society*. Los Angeles, CA: Sage Publications, 2018.

New York Times Editorial (ed.). *#MeToo: Women Speak Out Against Sexual Assault*. New York, NY: New York Times Educational Publishing, 2018.

C.J. Pascoe and Tristan Bridges. *Exploring Masculinities: Identity, Inequality, Continuity, and Change*. New York, NY: Oxford University Press, 2015.

Anastasia Salter and Bridget Blodgett. *Toxic Geek Masculinity in Media: Sexism, Trolling, and Identity Policing*. Cham, Switzerland: Palgrave Macmillan, 2017.

Shira Tarrant (ed.). *Men Speak Out: Views on Gender, Sex, and Power*, 2nd Ed. New York, NY: Routledge, 2013.

Nicholas Taylor and Gerald Voorhees. *Masculinities in Play*. Cham, Switzerland: Palgrave Macmillan, 2018.

Lisa Wade and Myra Marx Ferree. *Gender: Ideas, Interactions, Institutions*. New York, NY: W.W. Norton, 2015.

Index

N

O

P

R

S

T

V

W

Y